pause

How to press pause ● before life does it for you

Danielle Marchant

pause

How to press pause ● before life does it for you

Danielle Marchant

aster

An Hachette UK Company
www.hachette.co.uk

First published in Great Britain in 2017
by Aster, a division of Octopus Publishing
Group Ltd
Carmelite House, 50 Victoria Embankment
London EC4Y 0DZ
www.octopusbooks.co.uk
www.octopusbooksusa.com

Text copyright © Danielle Marchant 2017
Design and illustration © Octopus
Publishing Group Ltd 2017

Distributed in the US by
Hachette Book Group
1290 Avenue of the Americas
4th and 5th floors
New York, NY 10104

Distributed in Canada by
Canadian Manda Group
664 Annette St.
Toronto, Ontario, Canada M6S 2CS

Danielle Marchant asserts the moral right
to be identified as the author of this work.

ISBN 978 1 91202 309 7

A CIP catalogue record for this book is
available from the British Library.

Printed and bound in China.

10 9 8 7 6 5 4 3 2 1

Consultant Publisher: Kate Adams
Art Director: Yasia Williams-Leedham
Senior Editor: Alex Stetter
Copy Editor: Caroline Taggart
Designers: Nicky Collings, Geoff Fennell
Production Manager: Caroline Alberti

contents

Introduction

Part One

Part Two

Part Three

Part Four

Introduction
• • •
The Breath You've
Been Dying to Take

Today, for so many of us, life has become a running paragraph with no punctuation. Strive drive sleep repeat don't miss a beat. Our everyday stress levels and constant "busyness" are draining our inner resources and our love for life. We're off-balance, often exhausted; even our vacations only seem to touch the surface of getting back to the sense of who we really are. We might quickly feel anger, impatience, or frustration over things that don't really matter, or there might be an underlying sense of anxiety or low mood that pervades our day, weighing us down and keeping us feeling stuck without knowing how to get out of the pattern we've become accustomed to.

The consequences of running on empty for too long reveal themselves in our relationships, our work, and how we generally feel about life. We might lose our sparkle, have a short fuse, eat poorly, find it increasingly hard to jump out of bed in the morning, lack inspiration. When we forget to Pause and take a breath, things stop making sense.

The Pause is the period that lets us consider the next sentence in our lives. In that space lies the opportunity for reflection, perhaps transition or change, or simply an understanding of the next step. It is a moment in time to be still and to see what emerges. Imagine reading a page with no pauses. The words just merge into each other and nothing makes sense. There's nowhere to take a breath, nowhere to stop and reflect on what you have read so far, nowhere to absorb the information or story. Most of us live significant parts of our lives like this. A life which, without periods, feels overwhelming or without meaning.

As you go on this journey, you have a chance to **wake up** from the slumber of survival to fully experience the totality of your life again.

After recovering from burnout in 2012, I created the Pause retreats as a sanctuary, a place you can escape when there's nowhere else to turn. I created this place because it didn't exist when I needed it most. Pause retreats give you the space and time you need to just be. There are no demands. No responsibilities. Nothing you need to do, and no one you need to be there for. The retreats hold the space for you to reconnect with yourself, to reflect on where you currently are in your life, consider what's working for you, and make any adjustments you choose. In the space of the Pause, we invite the question that wants to be asked to surface if the time is right. Pause retreats offer a chance for you to be still in today's fast-paced world, so you can begin to listen to and trust your own wisdom above the noise of everyone else.

This book as a retreat

Not everybody can, or even wants to, attend a retreat. Sometimes the pressures at home or work are simply too great, or the timings aren't right. Maybe you don't want to travel far, or the financial investment feels too great, or the thought of slowing down and pausing is too daunting. Or perhaps you haven't considered a retreat at all; I know I didn't start searching for one until I had completely collapsed—I wasn't aware back then that a retreat could be a preventive measure.

If you don't think a retreat is for you, or even if you build regular retreats into your life, I want you to consider this book as a private retreat. A place you can turn to when you feel

Pause provides you with an **outline and structure,** which you can follow or dip in and out of.

lost, anxious, confused. Or overwhelmed, busy, and stressed. A place where you can feel supported and guided. This book provides you with guidance to help you slow down, tune in, and rebalance. Doing this will let you listen back into your own inner wisdom, so that you can guide yourself in your life in a way that is best for you.

Pause provides you with an outline and structure, which you can either follow or dip in and out of. It's up to you, and either is okay. In an ideal world, you would set yourself up with some quiet space while you contemplate the ideas in this book. Comfortable cushions, candles, and calming music. But let's face it, life is rarely ideal. Don't wait for the perfect moment to read this book; there will be few such moments! Find some time on the commute to work, read a little while you are stirring the sauce for dinner, or turn some pages until you fall asleep at night. However it works for you. This is the way of the Pause: We find what moments we can in our busy lives to take a breath and reset until the moments become a more regular practice and, eventually, we learn how to make them a natural rhythm for ourselves.

Remember, life is messy, but it is a perfect mess.

The Pause is the moment in which
we can give ourselves permission
to **gently unravel.**

So what is the Pause?

When we Pause, we give ourselves time to think and space to breathe so that we can explore how we make our decisions and ask if we would like to make some new ones. The Pause lets us take deeper breaths and gently understand the threads that run through our unease, giving the big question that needs to be attended to the space to surface. It is the reminder of all that is good in our life, what fires up our passion, the people who inspire and connect with us. It is the space in which we can relax, play, explore, and let new opportunities into our lives. The Pause is the moment in which we can give ourselves permission to gently unravel. It is a safe space to release deep pain and grief and open ourselves up to our inner desires.

If we can be open to listening to the messages our body, mind, soul, and life send us, we can learn how to notice them coming and develop the inner tools we need to use them as signposts. We learn to press pause before life does it for us. Pausing becomes a practice with which we can engage in the busyness of life from a connected place inside instead of a place of fear, panic, or anxiety. It becomes a daily tonic, a source of nourishment. It isn't always easy, because the shadows are just as much a part of us and our lives as the light, but if we are curious and observant, then we give ourselves a chance to return to our natural state of balance.

Where there is perfection, there is no story to tell.

– Ben Okri

Just as individuals will all arrive at a retreat with different energies—some wired, some panicking about being late or taking time off, others exhausted and feeling vulnerable, still others with a feeling of readiness—the same will be true about where you are right now as you read these opening lines. And just this moment of checking in and asking yourself how you are is perhaps something you are unused to doing. This is the Pause, because if you never stop to ask yourself how you are doing, how will you ever really know where you are going?

In this book, I'm going to offer you the process of the Pause as I do on the retreats and in my one-to-one coaching. I want to hold the space for you so that:

- You can slow down enough to breathe fully and deeply.
- You can find out how you are doing, what's going well, and what you would like to give a little more of your attention to.
- You can learn how to use your own wisdom and intuition to direct how you might begin the next sentence in your life.

I also want to give you a series of everyday practices that will enable you to take a micro pause in moments that overwhelm, and some longer-term practices that are designed to help you develop your intuition, understand your dreams, and nourish your energy.

It is important to me that you know my life is perfect only in its imperfections. Like you, I am on my own voyage of discovery. The unexpected twists and turns of my life have provided me with countless opportunities for deep learning and self-awareness. I hope in some way my story gives you permission to slow down, take a breath, and Pause. I hope this book allows you space to explore your own life, health, and well-being alongside me, and, if it feels right for you to do so, that you will join me in the future on one of the powerful Pause retreats held around the world.

I have been challenged on many levels, as most of us are, with family, in my career, through ill health, and as a result of my life choices. It took me some time to realize that all of these situations, no matter how difficult, were in fact windows of learning that allowed me to look deeply at myself and my motivations and to expand my view of the world. From the awareness I've gained in my own life, I have come to understand that in these times of constant movement, nothing is more critical than slowing down. I believe that unless we actively create natural pauses for ourselves in this hectic and driven world, we feel anxious, unfulfilled, stressed, and unwell.

How I feel when I Pause

To be honest, the idea of the Pause doesn't come naturally
to me. That may be why I am called to teach others about it,
because it serves as a constant reminder to me to slow down.
I'm someone with a big capacity for work and a strong desire
to make a difference as best I can. I have spent ten years
unraveling the conditioning that locked me into a pattern
of work.

I come from a line of women who worked hard. My great-
grandmother Olive had thirteen children. It wasn't unusual
at that time, but I find it difficult to comprehend how her
body withstood multiple labors and losses and still kept going
strong into her late eighties. I can only assume she really was
a remarkable woman.

Coming from a background like this, it was completely
natural for me to start work at fourteen while I was still at
school. I took two jobs, and so it began. The pattern of being
a woman who worked hard continued for many years.

I have been fortunate that, over the years, life has led me
to do the work I am here to do. Work I adore. Learning to
Pause has seen me refine and shape the way I live and work.
I have discovered a lot, especially about my limits, failings,
and being patient. I don't often enjoy these discoveries. But
I have begun to learn how to listen to life. How to tune in to
the bigger messages and instructions life has for me. When I
am busy and going forward full throttle (which is also needed

The **pattern of being a woman**
who worked hard continued
for many years.

sometimes), I am less able to hear these signs. The bigger messages and direction from life tend to come from a period of stillness.

These periods are often uncomfortable to be in. I want to "do" something—anything. Yet the more I sit with the stillness, the more I am learning when to make a move and when not to. I have a greater sense of the timing of life, and have come to understand that it often moves more slowly than my mind and I desire.

When I stay in the stillness, which can often feel empty, like a void, when I let myself be okay with not knowing what will happen next or when it will happen, then movement follows. When this happens, the clarity that comes with it is undeniable. I don't need to doubt my decisions; I am able to move forward with confidence. Until the next time I need to slow down and Pause again . . .

For those who can't stop, and those who aren't sure where to start

Pause is a book for the brave and the scared. *Pause* is for you if life has thrown you a curve ball and you're facing a crisis such as a bereavement, divorce, layoff; or you've had a wake-up call in the form of ill health. It's for you if you feel anxious, burned out, or are simply aware that you have felt unhappy or stuck for a long time. *Pause* is for business leaders and parents who live their life on the brink of burnout, knowing that the old way is no longer working for them. For teachers and health workers who feel overworked, overwhelmed, and experience constant anxiety. For creatives who feel frustrated or stuck, out of place in this world. For lawyers and bankers who secretly know this busyness can no longer continue, but don't know how to stop, let alone what might replace the pace. *Pause* is for the curious, the next generation who know there needs to be another way to live; and for all those people who are simply saying, "There must be more to life than this."

In a world that's all about pressing forward and doing more, the Pause is designed to help you strip back all the layers of "shoulds" and achieve the things that really matter to you in your life. Most of what you read here will not be new to you; after all, the essence of the Pause is simple, and isn't the world complicated enough? I know that you might already know what you need to do, but I understand that doing it when life is so busy is not easy.

overwhelmed

frustrated

stuck

boredom

drained

anxious

unfulfilled

lost

ready

crisis

ambivalent

"There must be **more** to
life than this."

This book has been written to help you give yourself permission to Pause, breathe, and reset. Even by slowing down just a little, you can bring about small shifts in your inner world. As the noise within starts to quieten, the world around you reflects this. Life becomes less of a struggle, and everything flows more fluidly. The Pause let you live the life you want now instead of the one you endlessly fantasize about. Learning to Pause helps you to feel clearer and freer. Big decisions become less overwhelming and more manageable. The stiller you become, the easier it is to access your intuition and the more you can flow instead of fight with life. Contemplation of questions you would usually want to ignore while living in panic mode, and time focused just on your needs, allow for a growing acceptance of where you currently are in your life. This, in turn, leads to an awareness and understanding of what you need.

Blending head, heart, body, emotion, and spirit, the Pause invites you to tune back into your intuition and be guided by both life and your own inner wisdom. As you go on this journey, you have a chance to wake up from the slumber of survival to experience the totality of your life again. Learning to say no, doing the things that make you feel good, and not doing the things that don't make you feel good—these are not self-indulgent. Listening to your own heart and wisdom doesn't make you selfish; slowing down to appreciate your life isn't lazy or unambitious. It is an ancient message, but still just as strong: When you Pause to take care of yourself and your own life, you become the person you were always meant to be.

Part One

• • •

The Power of Pause

I am standing in a field with my singing bowl in one hand
and paintbrushes in the other. In this moment, I realize this is
the Pause. This is where Nature holds us, spirit guides us, and
creativity fires us. This is where we let ourselves play again,
sit by the water and paint a stone, nourish ourselves with
good food, rebalance, dig in the soil, and feel the cool breeze
on our skin . . .

The philosophy of the Pause is simple: The busier life gets
and the more chaotic the world becomes, the more we need to
have pit stops in our lives to double-check we're on the right
path. The Pause is a deep inhale that lets us reconnect to
ourselves, and an exhale that lets us listen to our own wisdom.
It is a place of reflection, connection, and making sense. I'm
going to support you to listen more deeply to yourself than you
ever have before.

It's easy to be swept into the busyness of life and to get so
caught up being all things to everybody that we forget who we
are, why we're here, and what our heart yearns for. But the
truth is, if you don't stop and Pause, life will do it for you.

what's big in your life?

The idea of the Pause is not to tell you what to do, or how you should be, but to allow you space and time to shift your focus from the external schedule of your daily life to help you listen to and then follow your internal rhythms, intuition, and instincts. Instead of telling you how you should or should not live, the Pause encourages you ask your own questions. Questions such as:

- What do I need?
- What makes me happy?
- How do I express myself in the world?
- What is my connection to my community?
- What is happening with my health?
- How do I create balance for myself?

These are big questions, which, when you are trying to keep up with the external schedule of life, don't always get attended to. They become secondary to other questions, such as:

- How do I pay the mortgage this month?
- How can I spend more time with the kids?
- Who's going to do the shopping?

If we address the bigger questions, they seem to present more challenges—after all, truth calls us to action—and, because of this, we often brush them to one side.

The Pause is an invitation to attend to your big questions. Consider this book as a guide to help you navigate them. It is a way to help you create more flow in your outer world by listening more carefully and attending to your inner world. The essence of the Pause is discovery. It is a moment in time when a new understanding emerges. A moment when we slow down enough to be able to listen, not just to the incessant mind chatter and noise of everyday life, but to the deep wisdom of our soul.

There are two ways we can begin to do this. The first is by answering some journal questions and the second is by completing a short quiz.

Journaling

Let's look at the journal questions first. If you have journaled before, you can simply get started; if it's new to you, here's how it works.

First of all, you will need a book to write in, or a folder on your computer where you keep your journal entries. Journaling is different to writing a diary. It isn't something you have to do every day. When you do journal, you can take your time; there's no hurry—you're not looking for an end result or a specific answer. Don't force yourself to get to the end and finish quickly. Imagine that if you listened to the breeze, you could hear it speaking to you. Encouraging you with gentle whispers as it brushes against your skin. Luxuriate in sharing your story with yourself, taking the time to hear what needs to be heard from within. You can use journaling as a way of reflecting on your life and being able to hear your own story at any time.

To do this, it helps to have some questions, journal prompts to get started so you're not faced with a blank page. On the facing page are some suggestions. You don't need to answer them all at once. You could take one a month and see where that leads you. Do what feels best for you, and if these aren't the questions you need, create your own.

● ● ● How am I feeling?

● ● ● What am I grateful for right now?

● ● ● Who or what has captured my heart?

● ● ● What excites me?

● ● ● Where is patience required in my life?

● ● ● What's stirring my anger?

● ● ● What's new for me? What's old?

● ● ● What I want is . . .

● ● ● It's time to let go of . . .

● ● ● I am hiding from . . .

● ● ● It's time to let in more . . .

● ● ● My heart longs for . . .

Three tips for creative journaling

Journal with friends

You don't have to journal alone. You may find you have friends who are happy to gather and journal together in the evenings or on the weekend.

Journal outside

You don't always have to journal inside. Why not be inspired by Nature and take your journal down into the woods, to the top of a hill, or by a lake?

Let go of what you express

You don't have to keep your journal entries. You might like to sit and journal by the light of the fire and then create a ceremony to release the words into the flames.

Finally, don't try to force this (or any part of the process). Like a good coffee, or a profound coaching session, insights can take time to percolate and often reveal themselves long after the exercise itself has been completed.

the pause questionnaire

● ● ●

Along with the journal questions (see page 29),
you can also explore where you are in life with
this test. It is designed to help you determine how
ready you are to Pause in your life right now.

Are you ready to press pause?

	Often	Sometimes	Never
1. I am easily upset by small things	○	○	○
2. I often try to please other people	○	○	○
3. I find it hard to breathe or breathe excessively	○	○	○
4. I feel impatient if I'm delayed	○	○	○
5. I often feel lonely	○	○	○
6. I feel refreshed when I wake up	○	○	○
7. I worry what other people think of me	○	○	○
8. I wake up naturally in the morning	○	○	○
9. I spend good quality time with my friends	○	○	○
10. I worry about how things will turn out	○	○	○
11. I check my phone compulsively	○	○	○

	Often	Sometimes	Never
12. I am able to turn off my technology for the entire weekend	◯	◯	◯
13. I compare my life to the stories I read on social media	◯	◯	◯
14. I feel I lead a life with purpose	◯	◯	◯
15. I worry about money	◯	◯	◯
16. I can let my mistakes go easily	◯	◯	◯
17. I feel comfortable with the way I look	◯	◯	◯
18. I feel full of energy	◯	◯	◯
19. I fall asleep on the couch before bedtime	◯	◯	◯
20. I dream of a radically different life	◯	◯	◯

As you respond to these statements, you may begin to feel a sense of the degree to which you are ready to Pause; if you haven't seen signs before, some of them may become apparent. Take some time to consider why some statements resonate with you more than others. You are your own best guide here.

the pause questionnaire
● ● ●

Your scores

		Often	Sometimes	Never
1.	I am easily upset by small things	2	1	0
2.	I often try to please other people	2	1	0
3.	I find it hard to breathe or breathe excessively	2	1	0
4.	I feel impatient if I'm delayed	2	1	0
5.	I often feel lonely	2	1	0
6.	I feel refreshed when I wake up	0	1	2
7.	I worry what other people think of me	2	1	0
8.	I wake up naturally in the morning	0	1	2
9.	I spend good quality time with my friends	0	1	2
10.	I worry about how things will turn out	2	1	0
11.	I check my phone compulsively	2	1	0
12.	I am able to turn off my technology for the entire weekend	0	1	2
13.	I compare my life to the stories I read on social media	2	1	0
14.	I feel I lead a life with purpose	0	1	2
15.	I worry about money	2	1	0
16.	I can let my mistakes go easily	0	1	2
17.	I feel comfortable with the way I look	0	1	2
18.	I feel full of energy	0	1	2
19.	I fall asleep on the couch before bedtime	2	1	0
20.	I dream of a radically different life	2	1	0

Your results

0–10

If you scored 0 for many of your answers, you are taking good care of yourself and your emotions at this time; perhaps you have developed your own practices for nourishing your energy and giving yourself time to turn off. If you scored 1 or 2 for any answers, you may want to keep these questions in mind as you read through the Pause process, because it is the perfect opportunity to address any areas of your life that feel overwhelming, frustrating, or disappointing. It is not a case of "fixing" these areas; it's more about exploring and asking yourself what you need, which may include considering what it is you want to give.

11–20

You may be experiencing specific signs, such as struggling to enjoy a peaceful night's sleep, or you may be generally okay, but not quite firing on all cylinders. Sometimes, it is easier to Pause when you know you are in a crisis, when you literally can't get out of bed in the morning, whereas you may be going to work every day, with everything on the surface seemingly good in your life, while having a nagging sense of unease beneath. It feels selfish to complain, but you can't seem to stop worrying about what might go wrong, or you just don't feel passionate anymore. This is your opportunity to Pause before life does it for you. Do you really want to be on autopilot at this time in your life? What are you waiting for? What are

the pause questionnaire

you afraid of? As you go through the Pause process, be ready for some uncomfortable questions to rise up, but recognize that they are keys to opening up your horizons and beginning new adventures without those heavy weights you are carrying around with you.

21–40

The signs are there for you: Your body and/or your heart are showing you it is time to give yourself permission to take better care of yourself, to give yourself some space. It might be frightening to think of spending time alone with yourself, with no phone to constantly check, with a blank page. You might know deep down that you need this, but you're also worried that Pausing is just setting yourself up for more disappointment, confusion, or heartache. That keeping going is the one thing that is keeping you from falling apart. I know this feeling all too well, and I know how important it is to be gentle with yourself as you Pause and let your life slow down, to let what really matters to you surface and be given attention. Looking into the dark corners isn't easy, but it is what makes us whole.

● ● ●

If you instinctively know that Nature
is nourishing and grounding for you, make it
a priority to spend some time in Nature. If you
sense that your spirit is in need of connection
or magic, let your wisdom and intuition speak
up to be open to connecting with the energy
around you, to letting the universe guide you.
And if your creativity, your passions, need
firing up, be open to going on more adventures
in your life, whether near or far.
I would encourage you to consider these
three pillars of Pause—Nature, spirit, and
creativity—and feel which of them are
important to you. They may provide you with
support or a catalyst.

Express yourself, have fun,
play, and lighten up.

Who are you?

Over a number of years, I had stripped away layers of myself. Slowly, almost unnoticeably to the outside world, I was different.

Becoming less of who I was, so I could be more of who I am.

It should have been a celebration.

So much to be thankful for.

Facing the shadows of the dark so I could dance in the light.

"I don't like what I'm left with," I confessed.

Being controlled by conditioning seemed a safer place to be than the emptiness of not knowing who I was without it. An identity that once was, no longer belonged, as I faced new realities:

- Family who were once everything, now fatally flawed.
- Ambition that kept the money machine moving, now ebbing away.
- Friends once abundant, now much more carefully chosen.

Who were you before you put on the masks, coats, or layers of protection? Before you conformed to expectations? Where have you wedged yourself into your life that you don't truly fit? Where are you out of alignment with what you do?

When everything we have conjured up around us seems so perfect—the job, the home, the partner—we can still be left feeling trapped. So much to be grateful for, but nothing real left to connect with inside and no sense of freedom on the outside.

So why would we create these illusions?

In our own minds, we like to present ourselves, others, and our lives in neat boxes. Clear constructs that make sense to us about our friends, work, love, family, finances. On the surface, these constructs seem acceptable, but dig a little deeper and we often discover they are not connected to our own beliefs. Instead, they are based on principles handed to us by our parents, teachers, governments, employers, and society.

When I was in my mid-twenties, I bought a house. It seemed to be the right thing to do. At the time I had a well-paid job, a strong career path was emerging in a respected organization, I had a company car, and I thought home ownership was the next natural step. Certainly in the eyes of the society I was living in there was a consensus that this was so. Logically, everything seemed right about making that decision, until I moved into the house. Suddenly it all felt wrong. I had this constant feeling that I was living out someone else's dream.

In our own minds, we like to present ourselves, others, and our lives in **neat boxes.**

Looking back, I realize I had created an image that fitted society, but it didn't fit me. Within a year I had sold the house, quit my job, given back the company car, and embarked on a twelve-month, life-changing voyage of discovery, beginning in South America. That decision a decade ago changed the direction of my life.

We value our individual uniqueness, and we want it to be recognized. Yet, at the same time, we are social creatures. We want to belong. To feel part of a community. To care and be cared for. To be seen and understood in our difference. So how can you be different while still belonging? It's unusual to wake up one day and think to yourself, "I'm not this person anymore." It's more probable that you have had a sneaking suspicion about something that's been building over time. You have reached a point where you can't ignore yourself anymore, where the circumstances of your life show you that it's time to change. Letting that unfold slowly is a healthy thing to do.

exercise

● ● ●

It's rare that people come to me saying that they want to make a change because everything in their life is perfect. They already have an instinct about a change, even if they can't yet see the full picture. For instance, they may instinctively know that their current job is draining them day after day, but they don't know what they want to do that's different. That's okay. You can trust your instincts without having to make huge changes to begin with. In fact, sometimes it's better to stay where you are for a while and get some help to understand yourself and what needs to change instead of immediately jumping ship and creating a similar experience all over again.

It takes courage to be different, but the consequences of living a life that's not completely yours are greater than the risk it takes to be true to who you are. As conditioning slips away, so do people who don't want to face the reality of their own lives. As you shed skin, you shine more brightly and, as you do, you become a magnet for those who are as brave as you. The irony is that each time you question who you are, challenge the world around you, risk being different in order to be more who you truly are, the more you belong.

Do you ever feel a longing to be somewhere other than where you are right now? Not geographically, although you might sometimes long for distant shores. It's more about an inner sense that you're not where you want to be. A longing to feel more peaceful, more contented, while in your day-to-day reality you are anxious, hurried, and, at times, overwhelmed. From the moment you were conceived, you have been changing and evolving. Sometimes you were becoming more of you, sometimes you diminished so you could grow again. Transition fascinates me because I believe we are always in transition. People often talk about the power of change but, for me, the power is in the period before the change.

Have you ever noticed that when you are in transition, you are reaching for something you can't completely see yet, but have had glimpses of? A deeper kind of love, a more compassionate way of relating to yourself, a more powerful position in your parenting?

As you approach the threshold of change, you are required to let go of something so you can step into your new place. Letting go of beliefs, stories, assumptions, values, positions, hopes, dreams, desires can be a tectonic shift. But it is precisely these shifts that allow for change.

Stripping back who you thought you were in order to become who you really are—that takes true courage.

I often hear the people I coach ask, "Why am I not there yet?"

Life is a fluid process that moves like the ocean. The challenge is that often the mind likes to see an end point when perhaps there isn't one.

As you read this book, hold these questions lightly:

What am I stepping into?   What am I leaving behind?

nature holds you

Have you ever considered the enormity of the fact that the moon governs the tides? Our oceans are so vast, and yet an invisible force controls their movement and rhythm every moment of the day. The mighty ocean is powerless to resist these rhythms and has to exist in accordance with them. Research shows that animals do the same.

We humans have our own tidal rhythm inside us. In craniosacral therapy, the practitioner is able to feel the tide within an individual. The fluids surrounding the brain, which are there to protect it, flow up and down the spinal column. This movement of fluid has its own tidal flow, which, when we experience shock or trauma, can slow down or even "freeze." Being able to Pause lets us begin to experience the pull of the greater forces that surround us. This isn't just the moon, although the words "lunacy" and "lunatic" stem from *luna*, the Latin word for "moon." It is believed that people can show erratic behavior during a full moon. When women live close to the rhythms of Nature, their menstrual cycles are often in sync with the cycle of the moon. When we listen closely to our bodies, this is a natural time to Pause. Slowing down, going inward, releasing and then preparing to expand and go back out into the world. Like the moon, our natural rhythms wax and wane in a fluid way. However, most of us are living lives that are "always on."

These greater forces are not only the moon. You may also believe there are spiritual forces that influence our lives.

How Nature can help

Nature is a simple starting point to help you slow down and Pause. You can trust the breeze, the trees, the soil, and the river; there is wisdom for you there. The air you breathe, the ground you walk on, the water you drink, the sun that fuels your existence. Nature is the fundamental structure of your life—although many of us may have forgotten this and the deep sense of place that it brings. In that sense, Nature is the "container" that we live in—that holds us, nurtures us, and sustains us.

There is also another nature, the nature that is inside each and every one of us, our own, unique human nature. Many of us have moved a long way away from being in harmony with both Nature and our true nature. We have lost the connection to the rhythms of the day. Simple activities, such as the sun waking us and darkness preparing us for sleep, or being guided by the cycles of the moon, are no longer part of our daily lives. We use curtains to block out the daylight, we're kept awake well into the night with artificial light and televisions or laptops, and then jolted from our sleep by an alarm clock. Most of us have never even considered our own natural rhythms. What we need to sustain us from the inside out. It's rare that we pause and ask the question, "What is actually good for me?" We are less aware of our natural sleep patterns, we no longer follow our body's signals for food and water, many of us rarely move in the way we were designed to. There's even less attention paid to the differing needs we have at the different times of our lives. The result of this is

You can trust the breeze,
the trees, the soil, and the river;
there is wisdom for you there.

inner disturbance, and when you miss this vital connection to yourself, you lose what is important for your overall health, happiness, and well-being.

constant
low-grade
headaches

feeling
anxious

tiredness

inability
to sleep

stress

feeling
restless

low resistance
to other people's
coughs and colds

signs of inner
disturbance

Inner and outer reflections

There is an idea that is useful to understand at this stage. It's a simple concept but one that is not widely talked about. It is that our outer world is a reflection of our inner world. The more disturbed you feel with life on the outside, the more disturbance you are experiencing on the inside. It's why two similar situations on different days can feel so vastly different, or why two people can view the same situation so differently. Something as simple as going for a walk with a friend on a winter's day will illustrate this concept. You might see a myriad of colors and textures while they see only gray.

We know there is a lot of disturbance in the world at this time. We have seen global financial institutions, governments, currencies, and countries crumble overnight. Refugees are forced to leave their homes and vast numbers of men, women, and children live in life-threatening and inhumane conditions. We stand on the precipice of an environmental crisis bigger than we dare to acknowledge. Countries and families are more divided than ever geographically, financially, and politically. Terrorist attacks and nuclear threats leave us constantly concerned for our safety but feeling powerless to act. The institutions we once trusted no longer have our faith. The communities we once belonged to no longer open their doors. The food that once nourished us is as depleted as the soil it comes from. Wherever you turn, there is disturbance.

● ● ● Pause

The more you reconnect with your own true nature, the less disturbed you will feel and the more you will be able to engage with the reality of life, creating simple rhythms and rituals that will let you come home. It's important to remember that it's unlikely things will change on the outside—the world is as it is—but when you come home, everything will feel different. You will feel like yourself again, and you will be able to engage in your everyday life with a passion you knew was yours all along.

Putting yourself first isn't selfish, it's essential

It is easy to feel that focusing on your own inner nature is very selfish when you look at everything else going on in the world. However, looking after your health and well-being requires a devotion to self, so it's important at this stage to consider the idea of "being selfish." All too often we don't look after ourselves, because we are busy putting the needs of others in front of our own. You might be passionate about the cause—after all, many of us gain a great deal from helping others—but there is a line between serving and self-sacrifice. As this line becomes blurred, the need to validate yourself by being a martyr for the cause increases.

We convince ourselves that if we are this busy in the service of others, we must be kind. We believe if we refuse to walk away to avoid hurting someone else, we must be honorable. We convince ourselves that if we give up on our dreams for another, we must be sincere. We give everything we have to give and more. We give our time, our hearts, our power, our good humor, our gifts, our energy. In generously doing this, we feel more wholesome. Until the time comes when we have given so much that there is nothing left to give.

The message we're really sending out is "Look how much pain I am in for everyone else." The truth is, however, this is not noble—it is dishonoring, cruel, and disingenuous to ourselves. When we don't take care of our own needs first, we have to manipulate others to do it for us, which creates codependency in our relationships. At work, we give more than we receive, depleting our energy reserves and vitality. In relationships, we adapt to the other person, losing our passion and intimacy. In parenting, we give up on our dreams, losing our sense of place and identity. It's like a white lie that doesn't protect anyone. Tricking ourselves and others in order to project a positive image to the world leads to resentment, exhaustion, and a loss of connection. It's the opposite of the harmony, peace, and balance we desire.

To healthily serve people, we must put our own needs first. To healthily sink into intimacy, we must sustain ourselves first. To create a healthy family dynamic, we need to take care of our needs first. It's not selfish to put yourself first, it's essential.

exercise

If you feel as if you are running on empty (and so many of us are), it helps to think about where you are letting go of your own needs in favor of someone else's. If this is a struggle for you, don't try to change the world. Start with the basics in the sections on nourishment, rest, and movement (see pages 186–203), and build from there. Making your own self-care a priority is an essential aspect of the Pause. If you don't look after yourself, no one else is going to do it for you—or at least not to the degree that your body and soul desire.

- Understand what your needs are first. If you don't know what they are, you won't be able to take care of them.

- Remember that your needs change as you change. If you are in transition, reevaluate your needs.

- Don't follow the crowd. Most people you meet won't be doing a good job of taking care of their needs. They are not your role models!

- Let other people's opinions wash over you. Do what you know is best for you, even if it means being different.

- Remember this simple equation: The more you give to others, the more you need to give to yourself.

Nature's rhythms

As human beings, we are not designed to be "always on." We have natural rhythms that follow the cycles of Nature. Our internal biological clock, the naturally occurring circadian rhythms, work on average to a twenty-four-hour cycle, regulating sleep, appetite, and body temperature. For instance, during the night, when we sleep, our bodies produce a hormone called melatonin to help us slow down so that our bodies can renew, restore, detoxify, and repair the cells that enable us to function. This is followed by the release of another natural substance, cortisol, designed to get us out of bed in the morning; then we get another cortisol boost after lunch to see us through the day. Our biological rhythms can be affected by environmental factors, such as:

- Seasonal changes, including daylight hours and temperature changes
- Physical or emotional stress
- Shift work
- Traveling to different time zones
- Vacations
- Using drugs or medication
- Pregnancy
- Mental health problems
- Some medical conditions.

As well as this Western point of view, it is helpful to consider some Eastern perspectives, of which there are many. According to the basic principles of Chinese philosophy, every being and all matter contain energy known as qi or chi (and by different names in other Eastern traditions). Qi exists within everything and Chinese philosophy understands this energy to alternate between two "principles" known as yin and yang. Put simply, yin represents things that are negative, dark, or feminine; yang is positive, bright, and masculine, and everything in Nature is seen as having either yin or yang qualities. In the cycles of Nature, while these energies are in constant flux, they also naturally balance. For example, the seed (yin) grows into the plant (yang), which itself dies back to the earth (yin). This takes place within the changes of the seasons. Winter (yin) transforms through spring into summer (yang), which, in turn, transforms through fall into winter again. Because of this, the science of Traditional Chinese Medicine (TCM) pays close attention to the effects of seasonal changes on our bodies and well-being.

There is an appreciation that we are affected by seasonal changes, and that to best nourish our systems, we should live in harmony with them. To do this, we should nurture our yang in spring and summer and our yin in fall and winter. It's one of the reasons we often see people who live in hot climates eating spicy food, because it expands the yang energy.

Like winter, you are designed to be dormant. You are meant to meet yourself in the darkness of the shadows, and if you suffocate the dark, you block out the light. As a result:

● ● ● Your true talents don't shine

● ● ● Your innate gifts atrophy

● ● ● Your unique brilliance diminishes.

All starved of the fuel they need to flourish. For as day follows night, so light follows dark.

Five elements correspondences—Nature

SEASON	ENVIRONMENTAL INFLUENCE	DEVELOPMENT
Spring (yang)	Wind	Birth
Summer (yang)	Heat	Growth
Late Summer (decreasing yang and increasing yin)	Dampness	Transformation
Fall (yin)	Dryness	Harvest
Winter (yin)	Cold	Storing

❝❝ Harmony with the seasons is second nature to the balanced person. Unfortunately, most of us have blunted our instinctual awareness; only through practices that bring us close to the cycles of Nature do we begin to hear the voice of our own nature clearly. ❞❞

– Paul Pitchford,
Healing with Whole Foods

exercise

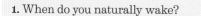

To understand your own natural rhythms, you need to let go of what you currently do every day and instead reconnect with what is actually best for you. Although these aspects of your life will feel familiar, the aim is to look at them with fresh eyes. Assume that you are thinking about yourself for the first time and that these are new questions for you. The art of this process is to learn to tune back into your instincts and awareness. Remember that your answers to these questions may have different responses according to the seasons, or they may remain the same. In your journal, you can create a table that looks like this:

	Spring
1. When do you naturally wake?	
2. What are the best times of day for you to eat?	
3. When does your body prefer to sleep?	
4. How much sleep is best for you?	
5. When are you most naturally alert?	
6. When do your energy levels dip?	
7. When are your best work times?	

These questions are not complex, but I want to invite you to look at them with fresh eyes so that you can explore what is best for you naturally instead of what you actually do. For instance, you may wake up naturally at a different time than your partner. Or your job may require you to be at the office from 8 a.m. to 5 p.m., when your energy levels are best later in the evening. That can make answering some of these questions challenging, while others will be easy. The object is to tune into your body to hear the answers that are best for you. Be patient. Living in your natural rhythm is key to being able to Pause and reconnect with yourself. Take time to explore these questions; you might want to take a whole year and look at each season as it comes around; if you have other questions you want to ask yourself about your natural rhythm, include these as well.

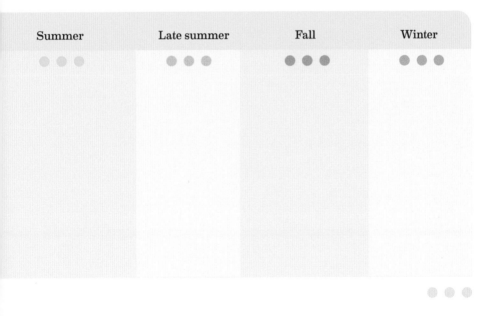

Summer	Late summer	Fall	Winter

Body and mind

On the Pause retreats, we use Nature as a way to ease ourselves back into our bodies, slow down our minds, and deepen our connection to ourselves through the breath. This isn't complicated, and you can do these practices without going to a retreat. The trick, as is often the way with the Pause, is to make the time and space for them.

Here are some practices we use at the retreats that you might want to try:

Micro/macro walks

These are lovely walks where we simply pay attention to our surroundings by zooming in and out between the vastness of the landscape and the tiny details. For example, as you walk, you might focus your attention on the sky and the clouds and then move it to a droplet of water on the edge of a leaf. The idea is to linger in either the micro or the macro, taking your time to absorb the experience before moving your attention elsewhere. Often when we do these walks at the retreats, people start to become aware of symbols and metaphors for their current situation in life; it's really interesting how Nature takes hold of you.

● ● ● If you don't have access to the countryside, you can still do a micro/macro walk in the city. Go to a local park, green space, or river, and find a path that feels spacious to you. Then do exactly the same exercise, moving gently between the open space and the tiny details— you will be amazed at what you discover.

Sit spot

This exercise is designed as a total technology break. It is not specifically a meditation, but it can feel like one. Find a place you are drawn to, ideally beside some water, and sit there for an hour without a watch, smartphone, pen, or paper. The invitation is to sit in your spot and consider a big question, letting it rise up but holding it lightly at the same time. You don't want to do this exercise like a dog with a bone; instead, the aim is to let the insights float in and out when they are ready. Whenever I say to people they are going to have an hour alone, they seem pretty nervous. That's because we rarely experience being with ourselves in this way anymore—we are always connected to our phones and social media. If an hour seems too much to you, do 20 or 30 minutes instead, and see if you can manage longer next time,

Again, you can do this exercise in a city, if necessary. If you don't have a lake or river to sit next to, do it outside in Nature if you can. Find a tree in your local park; sit next to the duck pond, or even in your own backyard or balcony, if you have one. Being in Nature will help you feel supported, held, and grounded while you do this exercise.

Talk while being listened to

Another thing we do at the retreats is to walk in Nature with a partner and talk while being listened to. The person you are with only listens—they don't ask any questions or respond with words. They are not there to offer any solutions or advice, but you will feel their presence as they listen deeply. You could try this with a friend and have one person talk and the other listen, and then vice versa. Again, try to find somewhere in Nature—walk along a brook, take a trip to the woods or local lake. Nature will add something to this type of conversation that you won't experience if you are walking down a busy city street filled with concrete.

- At the retreats, we light a fire and sit around it. This may not be easy to do in your daily life, but look for opportunities to be with a fire, either indoors or outdoors. It will stoke your spirit and often lets new conversations rise.

- We have also been known to spin like Sufis and howl at the moon, but that's another story!

Connect yourself to Nature through the breath

The breath is the pathway back to your body. Movement that lets you become aware of your breath will support you to connect more deeply with yourself.

Movement includes the physical body, and it also includes that invisible sense of flow of energy and emotions. You can listen to your body to understand which types of movement you may need at a given time. If you are feeling stuck and low in energy, you may need both gentle yin movements, such as qi gong, walking, flow yoga, or tai chi, along with more energetic yang bursts of movement, such as resistance training and cardio classes. If you use high-impact exercise to release the day's tension or invigorate your body, consider whether your body and mind would also like to have quieter, gentler ways in which to connect through movement, to breathe in time with the flow (see Practices for Everyday Life, page 182).

spirit guides you

What I call Spirit is an energy that runs deep within and around each of us. Internally, it is a spark, a flame, a passion, and a desire for connection. It is a need to know why we are here, who we are, what's the point. Externally, it's a powerful force that is almost inexplicable. An energy that when trusted and listened to makes magic happen.

In an era where logic and science rule, we have lost connection to our intuition. It is hard to define intuition rationally; it might surface as a strange resistance, a yearning, a niggling doubt. A whisper, even. How often have these passed into or through your life and your body? Did you take notice, or just put it down to "a silly feeling" that drifted away as quickly as it came up? Or did it linger, but you swept it aside, thinking it was wrong, only to be shown days, weeks, or months down the line that it deserved to be listened to? The more we dismiss intuition or disregard it as "nonsense," the more we lose the ability to trust it. The less we listen to our intuition, the harder it is to hear.

Think about how you are currently guided in your life. How do you make decisions day to day? Does your mind lead you? How much space is there for your intuition? Are you influenced by friends, family, social media? Do you have a set of guiding principles to fall back on? How tuned in are you to the messages your heart and soul are communicating to you? Do you ever let yourself be guided by life and the signs around you?

Now consider how confident you feel about the choices you make—both day-to-day decisions and bigger life choices. Do you have a place within you that feels at ease with the choices you make, or are you anxious when faced with alternatives, running different scenarios over and over in your mind, hoping that you can pick the path that is right for you, but feeling like a leaf being blown around in the wind?

These questions are not designed to trick you or to make you think you are doing anything wrong; they are simply a means of opening your mind to some of the ways you can be guided in your life. In the West, we're living in a time when the mind rules. This is not to say that the mind is not helpful—it absolutely is! It is a powerful resource, but it is not the only resource we have available to us. When we overindex on thinking our way through life, it creates separation. We forget that our body is telling us things, that our intuition has valid information, that our feelings need to be heard, too. We forget that there are greater forces around us, guiding us, teaching us, leading us. When the mind supersedes the heart—when status matters more than family, money is more important than Nature—knowledge becomes our key currency and as a result we're lost, disconnected from ourselves, our loved ones, and the very air that we breathe.

But we don't have to let this happen. It's possible to connect more deeply with all the resources we have available to us. In my experience, this requires us to slow down and create space. The mind operates quickly; it processes, files, stores, and deletes vast amounts of data second by second. Your body, heart, intuition, and life around you often (but not always) follow a slower pace. If you are in danger, your body will respond quickly, but for most day-to-day decisions, and even significant life choices, you are not facing true danger and this kind of speed just isn't necessary.

A few years ago, when I was recovering from burnout, I needed to make some big, life-changing decisions. During a three-month period, I began to notice something very interesting. I began to see how much farther ahead of reality my mind was. It wanted my situation to be resolved far faster than it was. In fact, it seemed that my mind was three months ahead of what was really happening at any given time.

This was a huge lesson for me, but remember it might not be the same for you. It can be helpful, however, to explore where your mind likes to focus. Is it stuck in the past, constantly going over old memories and regrets? Is it fast-forwarding into the future, wanting to move you out of your current reality and, if so, how far? Or maybe it is paralyzed in the present? Frozen, confused, and not sure which way to turn? Take some time to become aware of what your mind is up to.

When it became clear to me how far ahead my mind was operating, I began to concentrate instead on the immediate world around me. Over time, it became easier to focus on what was revealing itself to me right now. In fact, I learned, over time, that this was all I could ever focus on. Some people call this "being present," but I prefer to call it flow. Once we can tune in to events in our lives that are actually happening, we can respond to them (or not), which, in turn, creates a natural flow with life. The idea of responding to life instead of being led by the mind is not an easy concept (especially because the mind wants to be in charge). I'm not saying that you should totally disregard the future—it can help to have a plan. However, I was taught to "have a plan and hold it lightly." What this means is that you set your course, and then you dance with the reality of what is.

This idea of "going with the flow" has become more mainstream, and I often hear people say, "It must be a sign." Usually what they are describing is not actually a sign from life, but a mind-made construct. To really follow the signs of your life, and truly let yourself be guided by Spirit, can require you to face truths you would rather not see and make decisions that challenge you to the core. In many Native American languages, the word for "getting the message" is the same as the one that is used for "my life has changed." We have been brought up in an era that instilled into us that we always have choice. Yet there are moments of clarity when the truth is revealed, Spirit guides us, and we know there is no choice. We know what we have to do, or what we need to let go of, and that there really is no other option. We also know that life will be fundamentally different as a result. It's what I call a "no-choice choice." The times I've followed these moments of complete clarity have not been easy, but they are the times when I have found the most freedom.

If you can tune into the clues that you are presented with and walk through doors that are metaphorically open instead of closed, then you begin to flow instead of fight with life. It makes it a much easier journey.

Are you ready to learn how to flow?

This idea of "going with the flow" has become more mainstream, and I often hear people say, **"It must be a sign."**

exercise

Bee Meditation

One of the ways we can begin to create harmony with our outer world is to create harmony within ourselves. There are different approaches to this. One is creating a natural rhythm (with your food, sleep, work, and so on); another is learning to manage your mind. A long time ago, I was taught, "You have a mind but you are not your mind." In the same way as you have an arm, but you don't let your arm rule the show, why would you let your mind take over?

If your stress levels feel unmanageable and you find it hard to turn off and relax, your mind is probably busy. For some people, this is particularly easy to spot at night, when after an intense day they lie in bed exhausted, but unable to sleep. The more stress builds within us, the less easy it is for us to flow in our lives.

One tool that helps deal with everyday stress and lets you begin to manage your mind, bringing it back into harmony, is meditation. I meet a lot of people in my coaching practice who tell me that they have tried mediation, but they found it too difficult and have given up. The trouble is, when they sit down to meditate, they can hear their busy minds racing, and they think they are meditating incorrectly. In truth, sitting down to meditate will make you conscious of what is already present, and if, for you, that's a racing mind and anxiety, then that is what you will experience. This doesn't mean you are not doing it right; it simply means that this is what your inner world feels like at this moment in time (and perhaps beyond this moment). The art of meditation is to sit with the experience you are having, whatever it is, without trying to change it, judge it, or fix it. Your "job" in meditation is to stay seated and simply pay attention to your breathing while your mind chatters and your feelings come to the surface.

If that feels too difficult for you at this time, you might want to try the Bee Meditation (see page 74), which I describe as a meditation for people who can't meditate. I find it works well when you have a busy mind, because the sound you make is a distraction—and the mind loves a distraction. It works by blocking out the senses of sight and sound and creating an internal vibration by humming. The hum makes a sound like a bee buzzing, hence the name.

Here is how the Bee Meditation works (read through this completely before you begin):

- Prepare yourself by finding a place you can be alone for a few minutes. Sit in a comfortable position, with your back straight.

- Scan your body and notice how you are feeling.

- When you are ready, close your eyes, put your thumbs in your ears, and gently cover your eyes with your index fingers (the idea is to block out the senses of sight and sound for a moment).

- Inhale, and on the exhale make a humming sound.

- Repeat the inhale and hum for ten breaths.

- - ● When you have completed your ten breaths, keep your eyes closed, rub your hands together to generate some heat, and place your hands over your face.

- - ● Gently open your eyes and remove your hands.

- - ● Scan your body again and notice how you feel.

In the nothing something happens

The void was vast. A space that stealthily crept in and compressed me with its weight. Heavy and bleak like the winter around me, I felt empty and lost. What should I do?

My inner compass spun around furiously with no north to anchor it. My normal reference points had vanished, there was nothing but space.

As my mind raced with ways to fill the void, I heard my heart's guidance whispering gently to stay with the space.

The discomfort ran deep.

I did nothing, sitting at home for days wondering what the hell it was all about. No answers came. Fear fancied filling the void; rushing in regardless of the time of day, an unwelcome visitor. I resisted, desperately wanting to fill the void, surely something, anything, was better than this nothing.

Yet life demanded nothing.

Continued to create space.

Inviting me to step into the void . . .

I've been up my fair share of one-way streets and blind alleys, but what I've come to learn is there is another, often wiser part of me I can trust. A part of me that can sometimes be a faint whisper, barely heard over the chatter of my busy mind. A sudden rush of feelings that I put down to nerves. A part of me that I often override, deeming it to be ridiculous, nonsensical, irrelevant, or unimportant.

The act of slowing down and reconnecting to what our heart wants and where life is leading us is a transforming experience—if we have the courage to stop, breathe, and reflect inward. Yet our minds like to rush to the answers. Preferring certainty over uncertainty, knowing over not knowing, and plans over ambiguity. This rush for the answers can leave us missing the question. We suffocate the space.

Yet the questions are the whisper of your soul. What is the big question that most wants to be answered right now but has been pushed away by the busyness and distractions of your life? It's longing for your attention, and as you let yourself slow down, and as the noise subsides, the whispers inside can be heard. It's time now to let them surface.

There's nothing you can get wrong here; after all, many a great discovery began with a "don't know." You can trust yourself. Let the question unravel. Ask yourself, "What would I most like to know right now? What needs my attention at this time?" Sit for a while and feel your breath as it connects you back to your body. It's been a long time, hasn't it, since you breathed completely? Let yourself feel the cool air entering your body. Feel it moving through you, letting your belly expand. Track the breath as it leaves your body, gently exhaling as if you're blowing out a candle.

The Pause isn't about finding quick answers, but about slowing down enough so you can start asking the right questions. The answers are usually simple. It's the questions that are hard to hear.

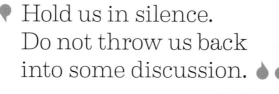

❝ Hold us in silence.
Do not throw us back
into some discussion. ❞

– **Rumi**

How does intuition show up?

Sometimes you will hear this wisdom as a quiet whisper
deep within. A call from inside. The part of you that knows
the truth, but you might still be afraid to listen in. The part of
you that knows your health needs your attention now, that it's
time to end a toxic relationship, or the part of you that knows
how you could express your creativity.

Other times this wisdom hits in a heartbeat, seemingly from
nowhere at all. You know right there and then what is needed,
what you must do, how you must act. It's unquestionable,
undeniable.

Because sometimes there are moments in life when you know
all you need to know.

exercise

● ● ●

How can you tune in to your intuition?

● ● ● **Notice the whispers**

If you hear a whisper or voice, or have a rush of feeling, don't push it aside. Give it a little room to work itself out and show you its card. We often override these feelings as worries or pieces of insignificant information, but after a while you may come to realize they are more important than that.

● ● ● **Pay attention to coincidences**

Albert Einstein said, "Coincidence is God's way of remaining anonymous." I believe there is something to be gained from coincidences that spark a feeling inside us, or seem too weird to be happening. If this stirs a strong feeling or voice, listen to it.

● ● ● **Respond to the unexpected with curiosity**

Sometimes your gut likes to jump out and lead you to things that you don't necessarily understand at first. Drawn to something? Think about why. What is your intuition trying to tell you? Respond with curiosity, and by that I mean don't try to control what's happening. Just flow and play with it.

● ● ● **Listen to the wisdom that lies deep inside**

I'm sure that if we got a dollar every time we wished we had trusted our instincts, we would all be rich. Hindsight is a wonderful thing. Try to avoid those moments of regret by tuning in next time. When you catch a whisper, ask it to repeat itself and to speak more clearly. Your wisdom deep inside will always be your strongest leader.

● ● ●

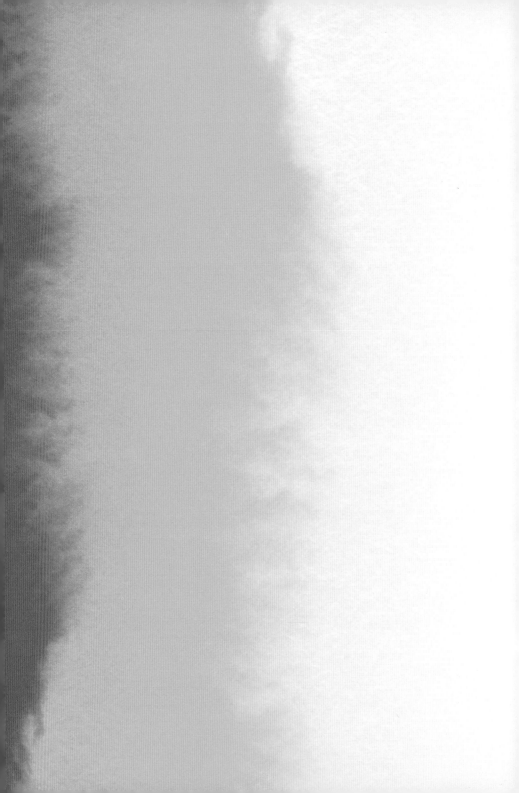

creativity fires you

Now that you have your foundations solid and you are flowing with life, it's time to let creativity fire up your passions. As you let your creativity flow, you begin to follow your heart and express what is within. This is the place to be brave, make mistakes, try new things, and have an adventure. Many people think, "I'm not creative, I'm not brave, this isn't who I am. This isn't me." Doubts like this are buried deep inside us, from the time you were tiny and told to color inside the lines and keep it neat, decisions that others made for you became beliefs. Over time they slipped in, unnoticed and uninvited, to become your truth. Yet the truth is only what you are able to see or believe at any given time. What if creativity was within you? What if it is within us all?

Creativity takes many forms, not just the obvious artistic ones. You can be creative in a science or in engineering, or in the way you approach problems or live your life. Often people say creativity has to be original, yet creative endeavors can also be an expression of something that already exists. What makes something creative is the expression that is uniquely yours. No one else, even if they copy your creation exactly, can make something the same as you.

One of the challenges with creativity is that it often makes you feel vulnerable. Expressing yourself and who you are, through art, ideas, or the way you live, opens you up to other people's opinions and feedback, which can be inspiring but may also be damaging. However, this is not a reason to forego your creative fire.

> ❝ Life shrinks or expands in proportion to one's courage. ❞
>
> – **Anaïs Nin**

If you can trust in Nature to hold you and in spirit to guide you, then your creative fire will not fail to expand you. The more courageous you are in expressing yourself—through your problem solving, your ideas, the way you choose to live your life, and also through artistic creativity—the braver you will feel. As your life expands in relation to your courage, you will find this becomes a virtuous cycle. Remember that creativity rises and falls just as Nature ebbs and flows. This is necessary—a time of rest and recuperation, preparing for the next wave of creativity to rise up. There will be times when you have stretched yourself to think differently and make significant choices or changes in your life. This in itself is an act of creativity, and at some point afterward you will want to let yourself and the energy settle. It's what is known as a "little death." Knowing when it is time to step back and let go is as important as the act of creativity itself. Shedding what no longer serves you (remember the "no-choice choice" from the previous section) and letting these little deaths take their course creates space for rebirth and renewal.

This is an important part of letting creativity fire you; remember, logs on a fire catch alight when there is space beneath them for the oxygen to ignite the flames. This is what you want: space to let your fire rise. When you let life lead you, you may find yourself in a void—a place of ambiguity, emptiness, and not knowing. Yet this void is a place of richness, fuel for your creative flame. Stripping back who you thought you were and being vulnerable, so that you can become who you really are, is truly a courageous act.

It's time to paint outside the lines again, to play, create, and express your own color in this world. It will look different for each of us. For some, it will be having the courage to work less and be a mother more. For another, it will be about daring to create a building covered in mirrors just because that spark is craving to turn to flame. For another, it will mean being brave enough to share how you feel about a situation.

Courage

Sometimes change comes crashing into our lives. A divorce, an unexpected layoff, a text that wasn't meant for us, an accident that leaves a space where a father should be sitting at the table. Other times change is gradual. Meandering slowly like a lazy river, almost unnoticed in the background of our lives. What if your courage were a quiet whisper, not a wild roar? What if it was simply you being brave enough to face the truth of a situation you are in and take a stand? To say, "This no longer feeds my soul and I know it"? To not need to have planned every possible scenario and outcome and played it over and over in your mind, but simply to take one step? One step that leads to another, that leads to another that slowly but surely begins to be a catalyst for change. What if you had the courage to change your life so that you felt happier, more aligned, more alive? What if?

It's easy to get stuck overempathizing with another person's position. Not taking the action that would be good for you, because you're scared that the other person will feel hurt or rejected or, worse, become volatile and vindictive. The simple truth is this: What is good for you is good for them.

Expression

When was the last time you expressed what you wanted?
What you truly wanted? I'm not talking about a bigger house
or a faster car; I'm talking about your secret dreams. The
desires that lie dormant inside you, desperately needing
breath to fuel the flames that have long since died down.
That place inside you that knows why you're here and yearns
to bring that to the world. That place of expression of who
you are. Your essence.

This whole book is a journey to help you reconnect to your
essence. To bring you back home to yourself. And now there
are two questions that will help you to continue your quest.
These are big questions. They are: Who am I and why am
I here?

Answering these questions need not be a quick process,
although you may already know the answers. If you don't,
you can spend your entire life pondering the questions, letting
the answers evolve with you. What matters now is that you
find a way to express your answers to these questions for you
at this time.

Adventure

The time has come to take everything you have learned and go on an adventure. I've guided you this far, but your next quest is yours to create. What do you most need? What will make your heart sing?

Yes, that. Do that.

I promise you won't regret it.

Part Two

• • •

Resistance

I've lost count of the times I've heard the words, "But I'm just too busy to Pause." And underlying those words I sense other feelings, such as panic, fear, and resistance. The badge of busy seems to be one that is worn with pride. Workdays extend earlier into the morning and end later at night. The working week now begins by answering emails on Sunday night just to get a fantasy head start. Lunch breaks are disappearing. Precious family time when parents can be with their children is being more and more squeezed. Time for rest and relaxation is saved up for the vacation, and even then the smartphone is never far away.

There is noise both outside and inside us. Endless emails, huge responsibilities, impossible deadlines, and excessive demands feed our already overstimulated minds. In the

Western world, we can sail, fly, drive almost anywhere we choose. We can virtually connect with people around the globe at the press of a button. We can learn what is happening in the world and beyond the instant it occurs.

Advertising fills us with dreams and desires for things we didn't even know we cared for. The media divide us, filling us with dread and fear. We're addicted to social media, comparing and contrasting our lives with "friends" who in the real world are almost strangers. Politicians manipulate us, making promises to serve their own interests, constantly covering up the truth of their actions while crushing anyone who dares to speak against them. Underpinning this, Earth, our home, is fractured beyond repair. If you consider the idea that our outer world reflects our inner world, then the majority of people today are no longer living peacefully. In the busyness of your life, full of noise, chatter from the television and radio, text messages, YouTube videos, and tweets, you may think you are more connected instead of less. Living our lives virtually, through other people's experiences and thoughts, has become normal. Children being born today know nothing else. We are social beings who crave connection, but the digital world provides only a superficial connection. The more we move away from personal contact with our friends, family, colleagues, and communities, the more we disconnect from our feelings, body, heart, and wisdom.

The hidden message is the busier we are, the more valuable and worthwhile we are. It has been engrained in our psyche that to waste time is a sin. I'm sure many of you reading this who are energetic, hard-working, conscientious individuals will still hold a judgment deep within you that you're lazy. It's what stops us from taking a day off when we're sick, preferring to plow on. It's what prevents us from turning off our phones and dedicating our attention to the person in front of us. It's what keeps us crashing into bed tired but wired night after night.

The reality is we simply cannot healthily sustain this pace. We are sleepwalking our way toward a health time bomb. Eating fast food devoid of nutrients, no time to exercise, increasing pressure at work, poor sleep—all consequences of the stress of being disconnected. The World Health Organization predicts that work-related stress, burnout, and depression will top the list of the world's most prevalent diseases by 2020.

This way of living is exhausting. Look around you. You can hear the tiredness in people's voices, see the anxiety etched into their faces and held in bodies that barely dare to breathe. We call it living, but this type of existence comes with a flatness, a deadness. A lack of aliveness or spark. There's no fire burning bright inside. You end up going through the motions of your life without ever feeling part of it. Being a spectator in your own show.

Sometimes it's when we turn off that we become **most productive.**

Of course, this isn't a book about doing nothing. We need to function, get things done, and live our lives. However, there is a line between being busy and getting stuff done in a way that feels really energizing, and being "always on" and experiencing stress and anxiety without even being aware of it. For many of us, checking off things on our lists and seeing results provide us with a sense of accomplishment, but we believe that we are only as good as the things we have achieved; we are at the mercy of measuring our self-worth against our to-do list.

Given that most people's to-do lists today are virtually impossible to achieve, this creates the perfect storm for perpetuating poor self-esteem. Sometimes our accomplishments are based on fear. We may worry that we will get into trouble if a deadline isn't met, or we may be striving to do an exemplary job, but inside we are driven by the constant fear that our job will be terminated and that we won't be able to provide for our family. This type of energy is an "adrenal high" rooted in our body's well-known freeze, fight, or flight response. But we were not designed to sustain this type of response over time. That response was only meant to be activated when we were under threat. Today, however, many of us are operating from a place of survival, believing that we are under constant threat and on continual high alert. Heart rate raised, palms sweaty, digestion slowed, it becomes so normal that we are mostly unaware that anything unusual is occurring.

The power of the Pause is that you can get as much done, but expend less energy doing it. When we are in survival mode our minds become active. The harmless background chatter we are all familiar with, such as "What should I have for dinner?," escalates when we feel threatened. If there is a threat (real or perceived), our mind chatter begins to get much more lively, saying things like, "I'm not doing a good enough job, I'll get found out, I have to find another job." This level of internal pressure has many different permutations, all of which—if they are playing out in your mind—can sound real and believable.

When you Pause, not only can you reduce this pressure, but you can also bring your attention back to the things **that really matter to you.**

Why is slowing down so hard?

What makes it so hard to swim against the tide of busyness when we know deep in ourselves that it isn't working for us?

Imagine a situation like this: you wake up one morning in a happy mood, the sun is shining and even though you're getting ready to go to work you hear yourself singing lightly as you make your morning tea. Your journey to work is surprisingly smooth and you get there in good time. All is well. You walk into the office and you can feel the tension in the atmosphere immediately. Your jaw stiffens and the muscles in your neck tighten. Your heart beats a little faster and yet you have no idea why. All is not well. Then a colleague tells you there are going to be redundancies. No one is safe.

This is what's called a parallel process, which means that a group of people spreads a mood between them quickly. Sometimes there's a reason or a trigger that sets it in motion, other times there is no discernible reason, but the feelings are just as strong. If you zoom out from the example and think about this on a bigger scale, you can see how easy it is for communities, countries and continents to be experiencing a parallel process. It's conditioned through religion, education, government, media, and it's so normal we don't even notice it. This creates an undercurrent of fear, and often someone who is frightened speeds up. You can hear it in their voice: they speak faster and their breathing becomes shallower and quicker. Then they're on a hamster wheel, turning and turning and it's hard to get off. Even if you do dare to slow down, the risk is that, as you do, the uncomfortable feelings will rise up. Most of us don't want to feel the emotions we live with day to day. Most of us are frightened of these feelings, preferring to conceal and control them for fear of what might happen if they were allowed to rise to the surface. The risk of opening Pandora's Box is too great. What if the feelings came and there was no way of stopping them? No, it's far easier to just keep on going, to push through and hope everything will be OK.

What if this is just the way life is? It's hard and it's fast and we just have to get on with it. For many people this will be the truth. For most the idea of being able to find stillness in the busyness will seem too big, too far away, too incomprehensible. But some of us – you, perhaps, which is why you are reading this book – understand that when what seems important overtakes what really matters there is an imbalance. We realize that, in the chaos, the precious things we value are eroding. We can see this reality and don't know how to be with it. We want another way, a way that allows us to be awake, to fully engage in the reality of life and to do it in a way that we feel at peace with. Rather than judge our experiences in a binary way, "this was good" or "that was bad", we may become really curious about the events of our life. With this approach, life becomes our teacher and we become our own best guides.

❛❛ The best thing one can do when it's raining is to **let it rain.** ❜❜

– Henry Wadsworth Longfellow

Embracing uncertainty

Human desires are expressed in a myriad of unique ways, but when you dig beneath, the desires are often similar: belonging, connection, love, and happiness. Yet the twists and turns of life can be challenging. Unexpected bereavements, relocation, divorce, children, promotion, illness mean the path to our desires is rarely straight. However, much as we know this logically, we still fight against it, often thinking the path should be easier, that it shouldn't be this way. When events seem to take us away from our desires, we can quickly assess ourselves to have failed, gone backward, be stuck, or even be doomed. It can leave our desires feeling impossibly out of reach, especially when we have been carefully following a prepared path that we thought would lead us straight to happiness. As we follow the path, diligently taking our steps one by one, meeting obstacles head on with grim and steely determination, we may find that glimpses of happiness shine through momentarily as a minor goal is met. But the inner happiness is fleeting as the outer focus returns.

Over time, it becomes a trade-off. If I suffer now, in the future I will be happy. If I do enough now, I can bank it and be happy one day. The trouble is that "one day" never comes. It's a trap, with that permanent state of happiness remaining tantalizingly beyond your reach.

❝❝ You spend your whole life stuck in the **labyrinth**, thinking about how you'll escape one day, and how awesome it will be— and imagining that future keeps you going, but you never do it. You just use the future to escape the present. ❞❞

– John Green,
Looking for Alaska

Can't complain

All the time you imagine this future happiness, you know you have so much to feel grateful for. You might have a good job, a loving partner, wonderful children, friends, and family. There's nothing to complain about, so you mask your discontent. The upset feelings get pressed down and you simply get on with it. But as you ignore your discontent, unhappiness, or anxiety, you also suppress your joy and excitement. We have a whole spectrum of feelings, some that we perceive as positive and others as negative. If we suppress our upset feelings, our grief, sadness, or anger, we also begin to numb our joyful feelings. That's when it can seem as if we're sleepwalking though life. We go through the motions, hoping that one day the future will be brighter for us.

Happiness, like all feelings, is a moment-by-moment experience, not something that you have to wait for in the future. Just as you can't trade the present for future happiness, you also can't hold onto happiness. Like all emotions, happiness is designed to flow. It moves through you. It comes and goes. It is not a permanent state. The same is true for love and connection. You fall in and you fall out.

To truly be happy, you need to be able to feel the full spectrum of your feelings. This is what makes pausing difficult. As you slow down, the feelings that have always been present within you start to rise up. The hurt, pain, loneliness. It can seem that Pausing makes you feel worse, and who wants that? But as you Pause, I encourage you to welcome all your emotions, to fully experience them and let them flow through you. Because we are speeding up at such an incredible pace, we can barely breathe, let alone be a witness to our own journey of life.

Tuning out your loneliness means
closing down your connection.

Shutting down your pain
means denying your love.

Closing off your rage means
foregoing your ecstasy.

The question is, would you rather stay asleep or face the pain?

From space comes flow.

From connection comes confidence.

From permission comes freedom.

If you don't stop and Pause, life will do it for you

Picture this. You're getting ready to go on vacation, you feel excited because you have been working extremely hard and know you are ready to stop. The last week in the office is intense as you make your preparations to leave. The weekend is spent in a flurry, buying sunscreen, currency, searching for a travel adapter, and updating your e-reader. You arrive at the airport, slump into your seat on the airplane, completely exhausted, and promptly fall asleep. When you wake up, your throat feels scratchy, but you blame it on the air-conditioning on the flight. As you transfer to your hotel, your joints feel heavy and achy, but you assume this is because you slept in an awkward position. By the time you arrive, you have a headache and fever, but again you think it's just dehydration. By the time you get to your room, you realize that you might actually be unwell and fall into your bed fully clothed for a restless night's sleep. The vacation that was supposed to be a fun adventure is spent recovering enough so that you can prepare yourself for the next onslaught back at the office—and so it goes on.

This is not an uncommon story, but it highlights what is happening to many of us every day, pushing our bodies beyond their limits without even realizing it. Pushing ourselves this hard requires us to override our innate wisdom. Often our bodies are trying to communicate with us by displaying physical symptoms, but we literally turn off our natural instincts, preferring to listen instead to the incessant mind chatter that drives us to "just keep going." When we do this, we place our bodies under tremendous strain. Our bodies are designed to survive and we are incredibly resilient, capable of sustaining high stress levels, depleted nutrition, and minimum sleep for long periods of time. Yet, as the story above indicates, when we do eventually stop after a sustained period of extreme pressure and stress, the body's defenses collapse. With a weakened immune system, it can no longer keep fighting and we become ill. I call these times, when life comes crashing down, enforced pauses. They can take many forms—a bereavement, a layoff, a relationship breakdown—but they are a reminder that if you don't Pause, life will do it for you.

I first learned how to Pause the hard way.

It was an inelegant crash landing into a messy pile and, in the fall
of 2011, I retreated from the world for three months.

It was a huge curve ball.

I was a high flyer, running two businesses, living in Singapore—
I thought I was having the time of my life.

On a farm deep in Cornwall, England, in the emptiness of no contact
with the outside world, I came to terms with how sick I really was.
I then began the slow process of rebuilding my battered body and
breathing life back into my weary soul.

I don't regret what happened, or the events that led me to
that point.

It was the lesson I had to learn at that time in my life. The good
news is I'm usually a fast learner, and through the experience,
I came to understand that life had given me an "enforced pause."
On reflection, there had been early warning signs. Signs that had
been present for a couple of years.

In fact, I had ignored the signs for so long, life had to make them neon and almost impossible to miss.

For instance, my body had been yelling at me—I just assumed joint pain (and a host of other symptoms) were normal signs of aging. After all, I was now in my fourth decade, wasn't this just what happened?

No. I was deluded.

I needed to live in my fantasy world to keep feeding the addiction to my work and lifestyle, to continue viciously tearing at my self-esteem, and to hold onto the negative stories I held about myself.

Enforced pauses often happen when we are too busy, too disconnected, or too burned out to notice and read the signs around us. Life is always communicating with us, giving us warning signs when we're not on track, supporting and aligning with us when we are. The more we can tune in and read the signs, the more we can flow with the events of our lives. This doesn't stop major events from occurring—after all, beginnings and endings are the natural flow of life—but it does let us be more graceful with them as they unfold. Initially, the signs are subtle—it could be a gut feeling or something just not turning out the way we want it to. At first, we might not notice these subtle signs. We might not want to hear the message we are being given or we might prefer to live in the fantasy of a delicate web of story we have woven. Imagine, for instance, that you gave your heart to someone, yet all the signs showed you they weren't interested in reciprocating. Of course, it would be less painful for your heart to ignore those signs, but as soon as you do that, you're living life in a fantasy. The signs become easier to read when you let go of fantasy and stay grounded in reality.

Then there are times when one area of your life is going satisfyingly well and another comes crashing down. It's a rarity that the whole of your life is operating perfectly and you are free from either suffering or desire. Nothing is static. Even the most solid mountain is always moving, shifting, evolving. It is what Nature does. The nature of life is that it is always changing. Rivers flow. Night follows day. Seasons change. There is a continual cycle of birth, death, rebirth, it's unrealistic to expect life to stand still. We are all used to the small twists and turns of life. We accept the shifting of seasons, the ebb and flow of relationships, the ups and downs of our working lives.

Other times, it feels as if we are riding a wave of uncertainty, numbness, and anxiety that hits us in the stomach so hard it hurts. Then the subtle signs begin to turn into events, sometimes small to start with—losing a purse or wallet, your laptop crashing, missing a flight—and then more significant. Suddenly, out of nowhere, you find yourself in a place where a huge change beckons. Instead of watching the river meander by, you're standing at the top of a vast cliff staring at the deep ocean below. It's so big, so high, so scary, and yet sometimes so exhilarating, that it takes your breath away. Nearly all of us have those moments when life suddenly spins around on its axis. You could walk into work, thinking it's just another day, and find you've been laid off, that you have no work, no means of paying your mortgage, your bills. The fear hits you hard.

Or someone you love dies. You thought you had time, you thought you had forever. But death can come at any time, thoughtlessly, pointlessly, unfairly. It takes away the parent, the lover, the friend, the child— and leaves you shaking and lost, sobbing or dry-eyed, with denial, hurt, sorrow, and maybe anger. *How dare you die on me? How can you leave me alone like this? How could you be so cruel?* And you barely know if you are talking to God, Life, Fate (whatever you believe or don't believe in), or to the person who has died.

Then again, you could walk into your physician's office, expecting to be told you need to keep off the burgers, or up the exercise, or that maybe you need a course of antibiotics. Or that your child has some simple silly illness. But then you're sitting and listening to words from your worst nightmares— cancer, tumor, heart disease, operation, inoperable, hospital . . . In fact, you stop listening because your heart is beating so fast and your mind has gone numb.

Or you pick up the buzzing cell phone and see the text that is clearly not intended for you. Or you sit, weary and tired, after yet another argument, another fight. Or you are literally bruised and battered, the promises of "never again" having been broken yet once again. You know it's over. Even if there is no big drama, no big battle, the end of a relationship can feel like a splitting of your soul. Where there were once two, there will be one. Even if there is relief, there is also worry—how to cope, how to move forward with dignity, how to live a life alone, how to protect the children, how to preserve your own heart.

Sometimes enforced pauses are painful, soul-splitting, almost literally heart-breaking events. Other times they are a quiet resignation, a moment when you reach your own conclusion, knowing that your life simply isn't working the way it is. You sense there is something else out there, something bigger (or maybe smaller or simpler), something that will make your soul sing, your heart smile, your feet dance. But, just because it is desired, it doesn't make it any the less scary.

Why does this happen? It's really important to remember that enforced pauses are not a bad thing. It doesn't mean that you have done something wrong, or that you are to blame. They are a way of us learning what we need to understand at any given time, even though this can feel harsh and painful. Enforced pauses are not the only way we learn, of course, but often when we have missed the subtle signs from life, the messages need to get louder so it's really clear for us to see.

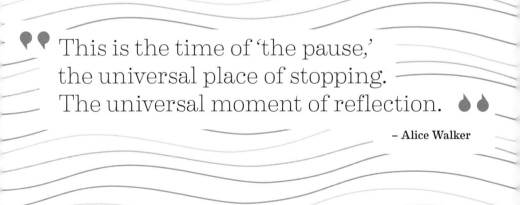

This is the time of 'the pause,' the universal place of stopping. The universal moment of reflection.

– **Alice Walker**

Part Three

• • •

The Pause Process

●●● Pause

what is working right now?

When you pause to consider your life, it is easy to think of
only the things that are broken. In fact, nothing is broken,
although I know that can be hard to believe. Amid the
turbulence, fear, and anxiety, you may find your body is tight
and that it's hard for you to breathe. This tightness makes
you feel more scared. Right now, it's important to remember
to breathe—it's going to be okay.

Breathe . . .

Before you embark on making a change, there are several questions you need to answer. Before you start looking into the future, you need to spend some time looking at the now. What is happening right here, right now, in your life? So many of us live our lives either in the past or in the future. Do you?

How many people do you know who spend their lives projecting out into a fairy tale? Are you?

"Everything will be wonderful when I lose weight . . ."

"All I want is to meet my soul mate; then my life will be perfect . . ."

"If I win the lottery . . ."

"If I could only live in the country/city/in a bigger/better house or apartment, life would be great . . ."

Or we sit and berate our bad luck or cruel fate. We lament the things that have gone wrong in our lives; we talk about our past bad choices, our mistakes, our unfortunate history.

"Why did I lose my job?"

"Why was she chosen and not me?"

"Why do I always pick the wrong partners?"

Sometimes the questions are almost unbearable . . .

"Why can't I have a baby?"

"Why did that accident have to happen?"

"Why did the person I loved so much have to die?"

Where is the present in all this? Lost. And yet at least part of the key to navigating big changes lies in what you have at your disposal now. It can be easy to forget the things that are going *right* with your life when you're faced with change. While there will be parts of your life that don't work, almost everyone has *something* that is going well for them, something that can be an anchor amid all the change.

Press Pause

I'm going to guide you through a mind-mapping exercise. If
you're not familiar with the concept of mind maps, it's easy
to grasp. A mind map is a simple way of downloading your
thoughts in an easy-to-see graphic way. Start off with yourself
in a bubble at the center of the page, and then map your life
out into various areas. For example, you might include:

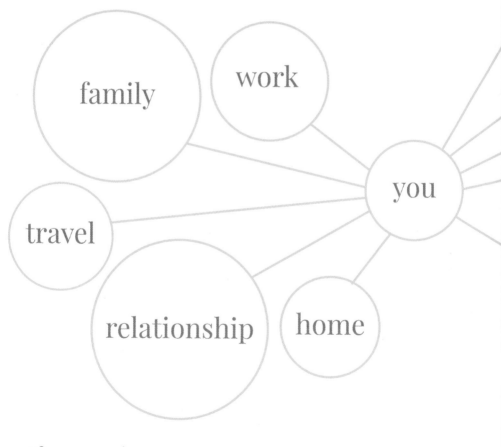

health

creativity/
learning

friends

spirituality

money

You may have other categories. Now scribble down everything that works for you in each of these areas. Some may be full to overflowing while others remain conspicuously empty. That doesn't matter. It lets you see that maybe it's not your entire life that needs an overhaul—just aspects of it. And it lets you keep track of the parts you want to keep. Although it can often be tempting to throw everything into the mix, you may run the risk of throwing the good away with the bad.

Look at your mind map again. What are the parts of your life that do work? Who are the people who do support you? What are the things that are worth keeping?

Remember to breathe . . .

Now take a long deep breath. And then another. And another. In fact, whenever it all gets too much, whenever you feel overwhelmed, I invite you to Pause and breathe. There is a whole philosophy and practice of breathing. Thousands of years ago, many ancient cultures discovered that, if you wanted to change the way you felt, you should focus on your breath. The yogis discovered that they could bring about profound changes in their bodies and minds purely by breathing in different ways.

But we don't need any fancy or complicated techniques. All you need right now is to know that, whenever you feel out of sorts, or scared, or lost, you can come right home in an inhale. In a heartbeat. In a breath. Just sit, or stand or lie, and feel yourself grounded on the earth. If you're sitting or standing, plant your feet firmly on the ground. Your roots. Let your spine straighten. Imagine there is a little line at the top of your head that is gently pulling you up. You are placed between earth and sky. Feel the cool air coming into your nostrils. Don't force your breath; let it take a natural, easy rhythm. As you breathe out, notice how your body has warmed that air. You have transformed the element of air, all by yourself.

Your breath is your home. It connects you with the world around you.

Breathe.

Everything
is going to be
just fine.

what do you want?

When asked this question, you may think that you have limited options, or you may be tempted to jump immediately into action and start planning and doing. At this crossroads, you get to write the next chapter. It may seem counter-intuitive, especially if your mind is in a panic, but now is the time for contemplation and remembering. Take a moment for yourself. Go somewhere quiet. Remember to breathe and give yourself some time to consider the answer to this question: What do you really want?

❝ When you are
dreaming of what is
possible for your life,
you should know that
anything is possible.
You may not always feel
it or see it, but you never
for a single moment
lack the capacity to
change course.

Your life is subject to
infinite revision. ❞

– **Karmapa**

❝❝ Our truest life is when we are in dreams awake. ❞❞

– Henry David Thoreau

Dream . . .

This is a good time to let yourself dream, ponder, and Pause, and to remember your heart's deepest desires.

Don't be tempted to race this part of the process. You're like a caterpillar going into its cocoon—you need to allow yourself time to grow, to change, to shift. This stage needs to unfold organically, in its own time, at its own pace. This is a time to let your fears settle so your creativity can flow. It's a period in which new insights can emerge, and the joy is that they can happen at strange, unexpected times. You may have a vivid image in your dreams, or have a sudden "aha!" moment in the shower, or find yourself smiling broadly as you wander around the supermarket aisles as a new understanding jumps out as you push your shopping cart. Giving the mind a break is a critical part of this process, so don't try too hard, or force yourself to find answers. Let yourself breathe and remember what it is that you want.

Your deepest desires . . .

You may find that you have forgotten what you want. You
may have lost touch with who you are and what you really
need. This isn't unusual. It happens for many reasons: maybe
you have lost yourself in your work, your relationship, your
parenting, or your caregiving. It happens stealthily, like
an invisible blanket shrouding your soul, until you can no
longer find your way back to you. Often, my clients don't dare
to admit what they want and need, instead focusing all of
their energies on trying to make other people feel satisfied.
It's as though we convince ourselves it is selfish to put our
needs first. For now, I'm going to encourage you to listen in to
yourself for a change. To let your deepest desires bubble back
to the surface.

Let your dreams surface

Most of us have desires that the mind says are "crazy" or
"will never work," that are "out of your league" or a "flight
of fancy." These wants and desires burn deeply inside of us
and never quite disappear in spite of our best efforts to
push them away.

After consistently pushing your wants and desires away,
it takes time and encouragement to let them resurface. You
need time and space to connect with these aspects of yourself.
As well as uncovering information in the realms of the logical
mind, you may also discover insights within your body, for
example, in your gut or your heart. A good way to access
these parts of yourself is through a creative medium, such as
drawing or writing.

Press Pause

I'm going to guide you through a creative exercise called free-flow writing. First of all, you will need to create a comfortable, quiet space for yourself and make it feel sacred for you. You may want to light a candle, bring a flower in from outside, prepare some tea, burn some incense, or open a window and feel the breeze. Do what's right for you so you feel comfortable and relaxed. When you are ready, here's what I want you to do:

● ● ●

Take a blank page in your journal and write at the top
"What I want is . . ."

● ● ●

Now, without thinking, let yourself fill at least two sides
of paper with whatever words come out.

● ● ●

Remember to keep breathing as you write.

● ● ●

Don't worry about it making sense or being coherent.
There are no rules—just allow the words to flow.

● ● ●

If you get stuck at any point, quietly go back to the
statement "What I want is . . ." and let more words
come out.

● ● ●

There is no end goal to this piece of writing. Just let
yourself hear what your heart has to say.

● ● ●

When you have finished, put your journal to one side and
sit for a moment. Take some time to breathe naturally
and notice now you feel in your body. If any emotions
arise, keep breathing and simply let them be present.

● ● ●

All is well.

what makes you thrive?

When we are under pressure or anxious about how our life is going, we often try our hardest to control things. We look externally, often zooming in on a manageable aspect of everyday life. We take action, any action, even if it's obsessively cleaning the house or tapping away at the calculator, over and over again, calculating and recalculating our finances. Of course, controlling aspects of our outer world doesn't provide us with answers, because the inner turmoil remains within. Frantically obsessing, controlling, or planning can actually take us farther away from our true self. We're not letting essential information about who we really are come out so it can be included in our decisions.

> I rise to taste the dawn,
> and find that love alone
> will shine today.
>
> – Ken Wilbur

What makes you you?

You, along with everyone else, have your own personal map.
The way you view the world, the way you interact with it,
engage with others, and participate in your life is in part due
to the values, beliefs, assumptions, and qualities you have.
Understanding your "map" provides you with a blueprint for
the circumstances you need to thrive.

Your personal values are an invisible and deep-seated part
of your map, and they form an integral part of what makes
you you. Values are often unspoken, but they will be evident
to others in your behavior. You will probably assume that
others share the core values that matter to you. However,
because each person has their own map, this is not always
the case. When your values are threatened, you will probably
experience anger, outrage, or a sense of injustice.

Look at the picture of personal values—which really matter
to you? Which are missing?

love

honor

connection

belonging

honesty

growth

justice

respect

service

freedom

loyalty

integrity

teamwork

fairness

It's not just your values. What kind of environment do you thrive in? Where are you at your best? Think back to times both at work and at home when you felt "at home." It's different for everyone. Some of us need to feel safe and secure at all times; others need to feel "out there" on the edge. Some of us like to work or live alone; some need to be surrounded by a small close-knit community; others thrive in big, bustling organizations or cities.

Shine.

What is your story teaching you?

Life is unexpected and change is an inevitable aspect of everyday living. Anyone you ask will tell you that their life has been a mixture of high and low experiences. Life is not a flat line, a smooth ride, or plain sailing. It is full of ups and downs, and change and uncertainty are natural factors. Often at times of change, uncertainty can make these periods seem like low points; however, once you have moved through the experience and have greater clarity, it is easier to look back and see that change brought with it great and unexpected rewards.

It can help to think of life as a collection of short stories instead of as a single, extended scene. There is no requirement for you to know the ending of your story, however tempting it may be to read those final pages. Instead, what can be useful is to explore the chapters that have already been written—in other words, where you have already been in your life—to uncover any clues that they may offer to your future.

The art here is to explore what the story so far is teaching you rather than recall every last detail of the myriad of experiences that make up your life.

Press Pause

To learn what your stories are teaching you, I am going to help you through a simple time-line exercise. The first step is to choose a period of your life—it could be the past year, five years, or a decade, or a shorter period of time, if you prefer. Once you decide on the time frame, here's what I want you to do:

- Get a sheet of paper and make a list of the months within your chosen time frame.

- For each month, write down any key events that took place. If you need to look at your diary, that's okay. Some people find reviewing social media helpful, too.

- Make a note of how you felt about these events.

Now get a fresh piece of paper—a big sheet, if possible.

- Draw a vertical axis on the far left of the page and another across the center of the page.

- The horizontal axis indicates the passage of time, the vertical axis is how you feel. At the highest point, you feel connected, happy, engaged. At the lowest point, you feel down, disconnected, and disengaged.

- Plot all of your events onto your graph so that you begin to form a picture.

Once you have drawn your graph, take some time to look at the story of that chapter of your life. What can you see? Where did you thrive? What was missing for you? What insights can you draw from this for yourself?

Looking back like this is a chance to see the bread-crumb trail. It's a way of starting to join the dots. You can't see the story that is to come, but you can understand the story that has been.

The more you understand what has worked for you in the past, the more you know what was missing for you in key times, the better you can get to know yourself.

Your time line can also help you make sense of why you feel the way you feel.

Sometimes, if life has been particularly turbulent, it can be easy to "numb out" in order to keep going. Survival. It's a useful instinct, isn't it? However, when we do this, we run the risk of diminishing or shrinking our experiences. Making them less significant than they were.

Drawing out your time line can help you come to terms with your reality. It can make sense of the past and show you how it has helped create your present. It can help you understand your situation as you breathe a sigh of relief that says, "Ah yes. I can see why now."

When you see clearly, you can begin to shine.

what is your reason for being?

As you face the reality of your change, you may think that you have no time right now for this level of deep reflection. You may feel that the luxury of submerging to the depths of yourself is for others, not for you. I want you to know that it is because of this change that you should take the opportunity to Pause and examine who you are. Life has presented you with a situation (or a series of them) that demands your attention, begging you to slow down, Pause, and reset. At the heart of this change, you are being guided to be more of who you truly are. It might be that you are being led to become the best mother you can be, or being encouraged to grow a beautiful garden; perhaps there is a story you are being requested to share or a business you are meant to build.

Your reason for being can inspire many or touch just a few. It doesn't matter what it is—what matters is that you know what it means to you at any given time. That you can reach inside and connect to your sense of self, and your right place.

This reason for being exists within us all, and will become clearer when you can look into your own heart.

> 💬💬 Who looks outside, dreams; who looks inside, awakes. 💧💧
>
> – Carl Jung

Awaken . . .

Being faced with a challenging crossroads, as you are, forces
a reevaluation. Now is the time to take the cue from life
to reexamine all that you thought you knew. You may be
experiencing nagging questions:

"Is this it?"

"Why am I here?"

"Isn't there more to life than this?"

In these moments of questioning, you might dream about escaping to faraway lands, meditating on a mountain, or being swept off your feet and cared for happily ever after. It's natural to fantasize, especially when life feels so uncertain.

The truth is, life is always uncertain. There are constants, such as night following day, but mostly we live in an unpredictable, uncontrollable world. And so to feel safe and secure with the untamed nature of the world, you need to feel connected to your place within you. To know who you are and your reason for being. Knowing this enables the world outside of you to shift like sand, while you feel stable, still, and strong within.

Press Pause

To help you explore your reason for being I'm going to guide you through a reflective writing exercise.

The question you will be considering in this exercise is:

"Why am I here?"

This may seem like a confronting question, but instead of making it feel pressurized, I will be encouraging you to hold it lightly. When you do that, answers will be revealed to you. So here's how to get started.

Find yourself a quiet spot in which you are free from distractions. You will be carrying out an important piece of writing, so book some time out for this exercise. You may even want to go to an inspiring location, a quiet corner of your yard, a tree in the woods that you love, a bird hide by a lake, an art gallery, or even your favorite café.

When you are settled and comfortable, I want you to write the following words in your journal:

I went to the Master and I asked, "Master, why am I here?"
and the Master replied, "You are here because . . ."

Now let yourself complete the sentence and then carry on writing. Let the words flow. It doesn't matter if they make sense to you or not. Don't censor the words, just keep writing. If at any point you feel stuck, go back to the opening statement and start writing again.

It doesn't matter if you believe in Masters, in gurus, in higher beings or not. Write as much as you can. Your subconscious mind knows what you're seeking and, if you open your mind, free your thoughts, and request this information, it will come. Be gentle with yourself, open your heart to the question, and let the whispers of your soul be heard. Let yourself remember what you most need to know right here, right now.

what are your aspirations?

You are half way through. How are you feeling? However you are is okay. You're will be joining up the dots between all you have learned so far. Take some time to read back over what you have written in your journal. Do you see any patterns? What are the common threads? What themes do you see emerging?

You may still be feeling lost and confused. If you are, be patient with yourself. You have been gathering a lot of inner information that will help you to reflect on your outer options. Right now it may all still seem crazy. It may not quite make sense. That's fine. Take all the time you need.

Sometimes we can stop ourselves before we have even begun. You may be looking back at your journal and find yourself shaking your head. "Oh, I'd love to, but . . ."

Put aside that thought. If you find yourself saying, "I don't know" and "I can't," stop for a moment. If you **did** know, what would you say? If you **could**, what would it be?

Review all the exercises we have done so far. Let them gently swirl around in your head. Yes, there will be contradictions. Yes, there will be things that don't add up. There will be thoughts that make you scared and nervous. That's fine.

Don't forget
to breathe.

Take your
time.

Trust
yourself.

❝ Create the kind of self that you will be happy to live with all your life. **❞**

– Golda Meir

Sometimes we need to play with time to find the answers. I'm going to help you take a walk into the future.

You are going on a quest. There are two parts to the quest. The first part is to open your senses, and the second is a writing activity. Your quest is best not rushed. Give yourself some time. If you can, allow for an entire morning or afternoon for your quest. You may want to choose a day on the weekend when you can really relax and have no other commitments.

Opening your senses

To prepare for the quest:

- Find a journal and a pen. If you like listening to music, check that you have a mixture of gentle and inspiring tunes available, but don't use it until part two of the quest exercise. If you prefer stillness and quiet, you don't need to find music for the writing exercise.

- Decide on an outdoor location that you enjoy. It could be a park, a lake, a forest, the sea, a hill, a yard, a river. It doesn't need to be far away. Ideally, it will be somewhere that you can easily get to by walking. Then again, if you need to drive there, that is fine.

- Read this section completely before you leave so you are clear about what to do; make notes in your journal of any instructions you want to remember and take it along with you.

quest exercise

● ● ●

Part one: Stimulate your senses

When you are ready, go to your location. If you are walking, you can use the walk as part of the experience. If you are driving, I would recommend you focus on the road and begin your experience when you arrive.

The first part of your quest is designed to stimulate your senses to help you access your creativity. Here is what I suggest you do:

● ● ● **Smell**

I want you to go on a "scent safari." Some smells reconnect you to memories and evoke emotions. How do you respond to such scents as cut grass, gasoline, warm rain, or a freshly struck match? Even just reading about these smells can stir a response. While you walk, notice those smells you enjoy. Freshly brewed coffee always makes me feel warm inside and I don't even drink coffee. Also pick up on smells you don't like—car exhausts, cigarette smoke—and notice any feelings that emerge. Remember you are stimulating your senses in order to access your creativity. There is no right or wrong.

● ● ● Sight

Now bring the focus on your eyes. I want you to look for three colors as you walk: red, green, and blue. Remember to look up, down, and around. Keep your eyes "soft"—most of the time we tend to look through "hard" eyes; we use our minds to work out the meaning of what we see. On this occasion, there is no meaning to be made. Simply look with soft eyes for the colors red, green, and blue.

● ● ● Hearing

The final part of this activity is conscious listening. I want you to open your ears. What do you really hear? Beyond the traffic and chatter, what else can you hear? Remember to breathe deeply and remind yourself that there is no "right" answer. You are simply tuning your ears in more consciously. Opening up your sense of hearing. What are the emotions in the sounds? Let yourself pick up sounds that are close by and then play with changing your range. Let your ears drift to the middle and far distance. Continue to walk, listen, and breathe.

quest exercise
● ● ●

Part two: Write a letter to yourself

Now you have stimulated your senses, you are ready to write.
Find a comfortable spot (still out in Nature) where you won't
be disturbed. If you want to listen to some music as you write,
now is a good time to do so. You may prefer silence or listening
to the sounds around you. You will be writing a letter in your
journal. It is a particular type of letter, written to yourself from
a future point in time. Here's how to do it:

● ● ● Choose a point in the future that is meaningful for you.
It may be a special birthday or anniversary. It may be
a particular year; it may be a particular age. There are
no boundaries—choose what works for you. It may be
when you are ninety years old, it may be in five years'
time, or when your child is ten.

● ● ● Imagine yourself at that point in the future. Where
are you? Who are you with? What can you see? What
can you smell? What can you hear? Imagine the colors,
smells, people, environment in as much detail as you
can. Remember to breathe deeply.

● ● ● Start writing a letter. Begin it "Dear _____" (insert your name). The letter is written from your future self to your present self, sharing all the wisdom it has gathered over the years. Your future self shares with you what and who you have loved in your life, what made your heart sing, what fed your soul. It tells you about some of the challenges you had to overcome to achieve your dreams, ambitions, and goals. It offers words of encouragement to your present self and suggests anything else that would be meaningful for you to achieve.

Take your time with this exercise—it is a deep and powerful quest. Once you have finished, there is nothing more to do at this stage than to rest. Make sure you get a good night's sleep; in the morning, if anything else emerges that you want to add to your letter, you can capture it. Remember, at this stage it is still not about action, unless you truly feel moved to. It is about a continued curiosity that lets your wisdom surface gently.

Can you feel yourself being able to focus through the fog? Let your aspirations float around you, whispering possibilities.

Aspire . . .

what would you like to create?

There is a natural ebb and flow to any creative process.
Sometimes you can feel stuck and unsure, and at other times
the experience flows freely. When you feel stuck, movement
is a great way to help free you. It can make you see things in
different ways. Why not go for a walk or a cycle or swim, or
put on some music and dance around your living room? Or try
some gentle yoga.

Yoga is excellent for helping us in times of change or reflection.
If you need more flexibility in your choices and options, practice
some gentle twists. If you feel you need to see things in a
totally different way, try some inversions. Get yourself up into
a shoulder stand, or bend over into a pose such as the Plow. If
all these are too tough, that's fine—simply lie on the floor with
your legs up the wall. Turning yourself upside down will always
make you see the world differently.

> Had I not created my whole world, I would certainly have died in other people's.

— **Anaïs Nin**

Press Pause

You will be creating a vision board. If you haven't done this
before, it's a fun, creative exercise that lets you consider what
you want to create in your life. Before you start, you will need to
collect together some things. You will need:

- A large piece of cardboard or foam board
- Scissors
- Glue
- Old magazines and any images you like, such as
  postcards, photographs, or quotes

As always, set aside some time when you can relax and spend
time with this exercise. Never rush your process. Prepare
your space by lighting a candle and burning some essential
oil. Peppermint, lemon, and rosemary all help to clear your
thinking, but don't use rosemary if you are pregnant or have
epilepsy. Put on some music you love, that inspires you.

You may want to create a vision board for a specific area of
your life: for example, career, love, or family. Or you may want
to keep the process expansive with no boundaries. Either way,
do what works best for you.

Now you can begin to create your vision board. There are
several ways of using this beautiful technique, but right now
it is about fishing, about discovering more about what makes
your heart and soul really sing.

Browse through your magazines, looking for images that have a "spark." They're the ones that make you pause, that call out to you. Cut them out and make a pile. Don't stop to censor yourself in any way. It's okay if you've never had the slightest interest in going to India but the picture of piles of spices is so enticing. You don't see yourself as the maternal type, yet that baby is just melting your heart. Never mind, snip them out.

When you have a good pile, leave them alone for a while. Do something else. You might even leave them for a few hours. Now sift through and pick out the ones that **really** call out to you. Not the ones you think you **should** like, but the ones you can't live without.

Are you surprised?

Our subconscious usually knows what we really want; what we really need. However, our conscious mind cajoles us, tells us what we **should** want, what we **should** do. Images can bypass the conscious mind. Listen to them. Let this be an intuitive process.

Arrange your chosen images on your board and glue them into place. Once it has dried, keep your vision board in a place where you can see it and feel the intention from it daily.

Let your vision become what it wants to become in reality.

Believe . . .

what are you afraid of?

There is a quote I love from the ancient Chinese oracle, the *I Ching*. It says:

It is only when we have the courage to face things exactly as they are, without any self-deception or illusion, that a light will develop out of events by which the path to success may be recognized.

Fear is natural. It's our mind's way of protecting us.

Sometimes fear can be the most useful and wonderful thing. It pulls us back from danger. It alerts us to bad situations and people. But fear can also hold us back from what we really need to do. Our minds can easily become caught in a spin of anxiety and fear.

Anything that is outside our comfort zone can get our hearts beating faster. We are creatures of habit—we feel safe in the usual places, with the usual people, doing the usual things. Sometimes we feel so scared of moving away from the safe and normal that we scupper our dreams. We prefer to stay within the safety of the known than venture out into the unknown.

Some of your options and choices won't look very appealing. Some of them will look pretty scary. That's normal. You are on the edge of something truly wonderful for yourself.

Dare . . .

Fear is excitement without breath.

– Dr. K. Bradford Brown

Confronting fear

Think back. Remember when you have confronted fear before. When you went to school for the first time. When you changed school. When you moved home. When you went abroad for the first time. When you went on a date for the first time. Everything is new at some point or another.

Press Pause

Get a blank piece of paper.

Take a deep breath; at the top of the piece of paper write:
"I am scared of . . ."

Now write out your worries, your fears, your concerns. Write
freely, no matter how silly or petty or crazy those fears may be.
Allow your fear a safe place in which to express itself.

Acknowledging your fear, looking it in the eye, is the first step
toward handling it.

Alternatively, if you're all fired up and raring to go, you may
be focused on exhilaration all the way. That's great—but it
can be worth pondering where you might encounter sticking
points. Progress tends to come from a combination of vision
and pragmatism.

Remember that the bravest people are not those who have no fear, but those who look right at their fear and then overcome it.

Remember to breathe.

Now, as you breathe, take a long look at what you've written. How true is each of those fears? How might you overcome it? When have you faced something similar and come through just fine? Where do you feel the fear in your body? Now . . . is it **really** fear or is there a tingle of excitement there, too? It's no surprise that the most scary things can also be the most exciting. Adrenaline is a powerful drug and we all need a certain amount of frisson in our lives to keep us interested, excited, passionate, juicy.

What if your fears are just stepping stones to something marvelous? Turn over your sheet of paper, turning away from all your fears. Now take a deep breath and look the world in the eye, without fear. Be daring.

Write down one undeniable truth about yourself.

And so it is.

who can help you?

When you're preparing to jump into the void, it can feel as if there is nobody at your back, nobody by your side, nobody leading the way. It is easy to believe you are alone and isolated. You're not.

You have people in your life, near and far, who can help. There are people you already know—and other people you have yet to meet—who can help. There are circles in your life, big and small, near and far.

💬💬 Leap and the net will appear. 💧💧

– John Burroughs

Press Pause

Let's take a closer look at these circles in your life. Get a blank piece of paper and draw three concentric circles: a big one that fills the page and two more within it.

In the center circle, write the names of the people to whom you are closest. The friends and family you know will stand by you.

In the second circle, write down the names of more distant connections. People you haven't seen for a long time, people who were once important in your life, but from whom you've been separated by time and circumstance. This could include former colleagues or old friends with whom you've lost touch.

In the third circle, write down the names of people you know who are connected to people in your inner circles. However vague the connection. However far away. However unlikely.

Once you have filled in the names of these people you are connected with, take a step back for a moment. What do you see? How do you feel? What thoughts start to surface? Sometimes we feel alone in our lives, and yet we are surrounded by people. Often we need to ask only one or two people for the support we need and movement starts to happen.

Remember most people like to help, it's the nature of human beings, and if they can't directly help themselves, they might know someone who can. Your network is out there, a glimmering web, and the strands are coming together. You may not know it yet, but somewhere out there are the people who can help and support you.

Your parachute.

Tribes

This is an interesting time. A time when people are coming together for like-minded purposes, for soul purposes. A time of deeper connection. It is no coincidence that the Internet has spread out its web at this time. It is letting us find our people, our tribe, no matter how far flung they are. It is letting us connect with those souls who resonate with us—those with whom we have deep, far-reaching ties.

In the past we were limited. Geographically. Socially. We had a smaller pool around us. Now the world can come into our heads, into our lives, to our rescue. Your tribe might be local but, equally, it could stretch right across the globe.

We are finding our tribes. The people who really matter. Those who listen to our goals, our aspirations, our hopes, our dreams and say, "Yes!," "I get it!," "How can I help?," "What do you need?"

In the past, you may have felt you needed to stand alone. To be self-sufficient, to be self-contained, to do it all by yourself. You don't. This is the time to look around and ask yourself who might help you with what you need. Your vision and your change might require skills you don't have, knowledge you have yet to acquire. You might feel that there are too many gaps standing in your way. The good news is that you don't have to do it all alone. Your people can help you. And, if they can't, they will know someone who can.

Once you start talking to people, the excitement builds. Ideas feed off ideas. Gather your dream team around you and miraculous things can start to happen. It's not selfish. When people work together, everybody wins.

Connect...

How do you build a solid, soulful support system?

If you still feel isolated or lacking in support, you may need to put more effort into building connections. Or even if you have plenty of people around you, you may want to consider the different contributions they make. I like to look at this from four different perspectives:

1 Physical

The first question to consider is who helps you to maintain your physical well-being? Do you have a walking buddy, a favorite yoga teacher, or even a nutritionist? Is the support your body needs more energetic? Do you have a reflexologist, massage therapist, shiatsu practitioner, or craniosacral therapist you can reach out to? If you don't, finding someone who can support you and your physical well-being is a good first step.

2 Emotional

The next question to contemplate is where does your emotional support come from? Who do you have in your life who is completely "for you," wholeheartedly on your side, and supporting your emotional well-being? Do you have a coach, a counselor, a therapist? If not, begin forming a relationship with someone in which your emotional needs are completely met. Don't rely 100 percent on family and friends for this—they will have biases that will naturally creep in.

3 Spiritual

Now you need to ask yourself what spiritual support you need. It's important to truly tune into yourself here and find out what your soul yearns for. Does the ocean provide this for you? Do you find solace in your church community? Do you have a meditation teacher who guides you more deeply to connect to spirit? Or does someone help you decipher the dreams you have at night? Let this evolve with you as you grow and evolve over time.

4 Playful

Finally, don't underestimate the power of play. Who nourishes your soul in a fun-loving way? Who do you call to share a joke? Who makes you smile and brings joy to your heart? Who do you have the best parties and belly-aching laughs with? Bring these people closer to you—after all, we can all benefit from a lightness in our lives.

One last thought as we close. I have been building my support network globally for a number of years. If this is new to you, don't think you have to do it all at once. Start somewhere. Choose one person. Develop the relationship, learn how you respond to their support, make sure they are the best person for you, and gradually, over time, you can build more people into your network.

what is your first step?

So the time has come to take your next small (or big) step. You can't get it wrong. You can trust yourself. You know what to do. However, I think you knew that all along. Remember, now you have a plan, to hold it lightly. The dance you do with life will lead you to your desires.

Dance . . .

You are at an exciting stage where you probably are feeling your energy to act building. You have understood your current reality and explored your big dream. In doing this, you have created a natural tension between these two aspects of yourself. This tension is vital, because it provides the energy that will help you to begin to move closer to your big dream.

It's not possible to choose the "wrong" thing. As long as you are focused on something that is relevant to your dream, momentum will gather.

Having many options can be overwhelming, so taking it step by step, focusing on just one thing, can help enormously. Action comes from intention, nothing is created without intention. So now you will be setting and refining your intention so it is the best it can be for you.

**If you follow the whispers,
life doesn't need to shout
at you.**

– Danielle LaPorte

Press Pause

As always, give yourself time to complete this exercise in peace. Start your session by breathing deeply and easily.

You will be exploring your intentions using some journal prompts. To begin, take a fresh page in your journal and, one by one, respond to the questions below. As always, allow a space for the magic to slide in . . . If something unexpected jumps out, smile and play with it for a while.

My hearts yearns for . . .
I feel most free when . . .
My deepest desire is . . .
I can choose to . . .
My focus will be . . .
This is important, because . . .
I can ask for help from . . .

Once you know your intention, when you are completely clear and congruent about it, it can feel incredible how everything around you will conspire to help you bring that to life. People will offer solutions. Opportunities will arise. It's as if you are an arrow that has been let loose from the bow—you fly toward your destination.

You have set your intent and every atom of your being is straining toward that end point. Your subconscious mind is full of the promised future. It is impossible to fail. When you are aligned, **completely aligned**, to your deepest dreams; when you have opened your heart and mind to your most profound possibility, then everything will come together. Your tribe will gather around. Unexpected opportunities will arise.

Keep your eyes and ears open at this time. Watch out for surprises, for curious cases of serendipity, for meetings and opportunities that seem to come from left field. Sometimes it feels like magic. You will turn on the radio and a song will give you the message you need. You will flick through a book and a quote will jump out and hit you in the solar plexus. Or, in a more pragmatic way, you will need something and you will see an advertisement in the paper, or someone will post something on social media. Be open to everything.

While this stage is far more concrete, more grounded and practical than those that have gone before, be careful not to forget the more subtle hints and clues. You are moving from the realm of mind and imagination, of dreams and desires, into a more physical reality, but those other worlds still inform and ignite the dream. Keep it light.

The world is a wonderful playground.

Even the most solid reality is only another form of energy. Remember that a stone and a dance are purely different frequencies.

Spin like a Sufi. Embrace the miracle of change happening in your life. Don't ever forget to dance.

how far have you come?

There is a certainty. That life is ever-changing. Snow melts. Flowers bloom and fade and bloom again. Clouds drift, expand, darken. Rivers become oceans. Tectonic plates shift. The moon waxes and wanes. As in nature, your very being has been changing. Take time to look at how far you have come. Where were you at the beginning of this journey? What is new for you now? What do you know about yourself, life, and others that you didn't know before?

Now is the time to acknowledge yourself, thank others, celebrate with loved ones, and breathe it all in. It is time to feel grateful for who you were, and who you have become.

> ❛❛ The more you praise and celebrate your life, the more there is in life to celebrate. ❜❜
>
> – **Oprah Winfrey**

Rejoice . . .

You may hesitate at this. It may seem premature. You may say that you have only just started on this journey; that you are still at the beginning. So why am I suggesting you celebrate already?

You have begun to set your intention in motion, but throughout this process you have been creating inner changes. Some small, some seismic. Step by step you have been realigning yourself back to you. There is so much to celebrate.

What are you celebrating? You! This is the time to acknowledge yourself, to step back, nod, and say, "You truly are an incredible human being."

Press Pause

It helps to have something visual to remind yourself of your intention, a touchstone you can come back to that reminds you of what matters. Go outside and look around for a pebble or stone, one that speaks to you, one that calls your name. Sit with it, turn it over in your hands, and feel its weight, its contours, its energy. When you have found your stone, you may find it is enough just as it is, but, equally, you might want to decorate it, to paint it, or print a word or phrase on it. Something that sums up your intention. Something that would remind and inspire you if you saw it on a daily basis.

Of course, one word or phrase may not be enough—you may need more. You may also want to make a banner or poster. Something that will pull together all the thoughts, stages, dreams, and visions of your change.

Draw or paint them out in whatever style, size, and color you want. Mix it up. See which words want to muscle in and be written loud and clear. Once again, there will be some hints and nudges from your subconscious just waiting to jump out. You don't need to be an artist—just grab yourself a pile of Sharpies or paints or whatever comes to hand—and see what happens.

Be thankful

Thank yourself, first of all, for having the courage and vision and sheer determination to have made it this far. Think back to where you were when you started. Look back at what you have discovered about yourself. You are an adventurer of the spirit.

In your journal, write down what you are most grateful for about yourself. Your qualities, your character, your traits, your attitude, your values.

Now look around at your tribe, the people who have already helped you; the others who will move into the future with you, holding you, pushing you, supporting you. Acknowledge them. Be grateful to them. Send a card, give them a hug, do what feels right to let them know how thankful you are to have them in your life.

Take a deep, deep breath.

This is energy transforming itself—from the vaguest of visions, from thoughts as wispy and ephemeral as clouds, down through the worlds of thought and intent, into manifestation. You are creating your new world. You are spinning it out of the air, out of your mind, and into the material world.

Do it with gratitude.
Do it wholeheartedly and whole-souledly.
Do it with love.

Part Four
• • •
Practices for Everyday Life

Each time you pause, you take a small step toward rebalancing your life and reconnecting with who you really are and what you really want. Accumulatively, these small steps add up to a healthy change in your daily routine that will let you function optimally in tune with yourself and the natural world.

There is something that is important to understand at this point about the Pause. Well-being is a daily devotion. Without these daily practices, over time your tank empties. Your qi (life force) depletes, and your finite resources dwindle. It is subtle at first—you might notice you feel cranky more than you feel inspired. Or that you feel tired more than you feel energized. Or that you feel low more than you feel happy. Or that you feel closed more than you feel open.

When you look at it like this, the devotion of daily practice makes sense. Your energy and happiness matter, and, if you don't look after yourself, who else is going to? How you choose to do it isn't what is important; that you do it is what counts. Meditation, yoga, journaling, clean food, supplements, therapy, gratitude, writing, getting into Nature, qi gong, tai chi . . .

The practice of showing up
for yourself each day.
Being there for you.
This daily devotion to you
is what lets you live
this life more fully—and
you're free to choose . . .

nourishment

These days, we often eat in a hurry, with our bellies tied in knots from stress, making it hard for the body to digest and draw out vital nutrients. Add to this processed food with high levels of fat, salt, and sugar, and it's no wonder you're feeling weary. Without good nutrition your immune system becomes weakened. If you're caught in a cycle of getting sick when you take a vacation, or simply picking up regular coughs and colds, your system is probably crying out for a boost.

Digestive health

It is well documented that your internal digestive environment plays a fundamental role in physical, emotional, and mental well-being. Maintaining a healthy digestive tract is also the starting point to protecting ourselves from disease. Paul Pitchford, author of *Healing with Whole Foods*, tells us that once digestion works better, all the other systems in the body can rebuild and renew. When the digestive tract is out of balance, a "damp" environment is created in which yeast, parasites, and fungi begin to grow.

Eat as many natural foods as possible

Not so long ago, we ate the crops we grew. Today, much of the food we eat is mass-produced, filled with additives and lacking the basic nutrition our bodies require. To balance this change in the way our food is produced, we're required to go back to an older, perhaps slower way of eating. Choosing whole foods that

are as close to their natural state as possible is a good starting point. Avoiding foods with more than five ingredients on the label, or ingredients your grandmother would not recognize, is also a helpful guide when shopping.

Eat seasonally

One of the ways you can come back to the rhythm of Nature is to eat foods when they are in season. Nature produces foods that support our bodies at the appropriate time of year. An abundance of salad greens in the warmer months help cool our bodies, while the dense root vegetables of fall provide our bodies with natural sugars for storage during the winter. Knowing when foods are grown can allow for you to tune in to Nature.

Eat mindfully

Do you check your social media feeds over breakfast? Do you hurriedly scoop in lunch while hunched over your computer screen or eat your dinner in front of the televsion? These activities may seem harmless, but when a screen distracts you, how conscious are you of the food you are eating? Can you smell the aromas, taste the layers of flavors, and feel the texture of the food? Eating is a multisensory experience, our sight and smell support the brain to give the digestive tract signals to prepare for digestion. Turning off these signals can slow your digestion down, leaving you feeling more sluggish and tired without even realizing why.

Essential oils

Essential oils not only smell wonderful but also have healing properties. Here are five that I would recommend keeping in your kit:

Lavender—A magnificent multipurpose oil, you can add lavender directly to the skin to alleviate minor grazes and cuts, or you can rub two or three drops into your hands and inhale for an instant calming effect. Add to your bath or pillow for a deep sleep.

Peppermint—A good oil to have with you if you work in an office, inhaling peppermint will give you an instant energy boost, or you could dilute the oil in some water in a small spray bottle and spray on the back of your neck or wrists to cool you down in the summer (or when tempers are frayed).

Basil—This oil is good for adrenal exhaustion and supports people who are feeling overwhelmed and fatigued. It is wonderful for giving optimism to tired souls.

Wild Orange—Naturally uplifting and energizing, wild orange oil is good for reviving the body and mind, and it can also aid creativity. Add some to a diffuser to spread some cheer!

Rose—This powerful oil is a heart healer for emotional heartbreak. It is also a wonderful oil to use during meditation to help you connect to your compassion.

sleep

Your body needs rest; it wasn't designed to be "on" all the time. Like Nature, who has periods of dormancy leading to rejuvenation, your body needs you to turn off at times, and the obvious time is when we rest is at night. However, sleep is not just about getting enough rest for the next day—it is a fundamental healing process. It's where your cells renew themselves; it's where repair and detoxification happens. Sleep is essential to feeding your vitality.

If your sleep feels as if it requires some fine-tuning, here are some ways to help you improve the quality of your nighttime rest and get sound sleep:

Before you sleep

Tune into your rhythm

We all need different amounts of sleep, and each of us will have an optimum time to go to sleep and wake up. Spend a week exploring yours. How many hours is best for you? When do you wake up naturally? What's the best time for you to be in bed; when do you naturally fall asleep? Once you have enquired and found your natural rhythm, stick to it as much as you can. Any small move away from your regular rhythms will have a noticeable impact.

Create an evening routine

Once you know your rhythm, the next step is to create an evening routine. The simplest habit you can build into this is called electronic sundown. Historically, we would have experienced the evening light decreasing as day turned to night. Darkness is our body's cue to prepare for sleep. Now our homes and offices are artificially lit, and "blue light" from television screens, laptops, tablets, and smartphones keeps us active long into the night. Not only that, but the content we are viewing also often raises adrenaline, spiking cortisol levels at a time they are not required.

Electronic sundown is simply a way to reset, which you do by turning off all of your electrical items 90 minutes before you go to bed. Then you can start to wind down naturally with a warm (not hot) Epsom salt bath and a normal printed book, slow your system down with camomile tea or turmeric milk, lie in the yoga pose Savasana (also known as corpse pose), or whatever routine suits you best. If you have LED ceiling lights in your home, turn them off in favor of lamps with incandescent bulbs, because evidence suggests that LED lights can delay melatonin (a hormone that triggers sleep) production by 90 minutes.

Take technology out of the bedroom

An extension of electronic sundown would be to turn your smartphone to airplane mode overnight (your alarm will still go off) or, better still, buy an alarm clock and don't sleep with your phone in your bedroom at all. The temptation to check emails or surf social media when you wake in the middle of the night can have a severe impact on the quality of your sleep. As soon as you look at the screen, your melatonin production stops, your brain wakes up, and before you know it the sun is rising without your body having had an opportunity to repair and rejuvenate overnight. Also make sure any LED lights in your bedroom are covered, even the faint glow of a television on standby can stop melatonin production.

Reduce stimulants

Coffee, tea (including green tea), carbonated beverages, chocolate, some medications, such as cold and flu remedies, and fast-acting painkillers all contain caffeine. While it might give you a nice buzz and keep you going when your energy levels are low, it can interfere with your quality of sleep. Alcohol and nicotine are also stimulants.

When you go to sleep

Turn the heating down

The body needs to lower its temperature in order to fall
asleep, so a hot bath right before bed or a room in which the
temperature is too hot will actually keep you awake. If you
enjoy a soak in a hot bath, take it earlier in the evening—two
or more hours before bedtime—so your body has enough time
to cool down. If it works for you, open the window a little at
night to regulate the temperature and keep air circulating.
If you live in a hot climate, use a thin cotton sheet and a fan
to stay cool, or air-conditioning, if necessary.

Epsom salts and essential oils

Adding Epsom salts to a warm bath is a simple way to detox
the body. The salts contain magnesium, which helps the
muscles and mind to relax. Remember that Epsom salts will
also raise your temperature slightly as part of their natural
detoxifying process, so take that into account when adding
them to your bath before bedtime.

Essential oils that might help you sleep include lavender,
bergamot, and vetiver. Try rubbing vetiver into the soles of
your feet at bedtime and sprinkling lavender on your pillow
(or mix a few drops into your Epsom salts and add to your
bath). Put a few drops of both bergamot and lavender into a
diffuser in your bedroom before you go to bed.

Pillow positions

Side sleepers, have a pillow under your head as usual and put a pillow between your knees.

Back sleepers, use a lower pillow than normal under your head and place a pillow under your knees to take pressure off your lower back.

Stomach sleepers, use a flat pillow for your head and place another pillow under your pelvis or abdomen.

Yoga Nidra

This Sanskrit term means "yogic sleep" and refers to a form of deep meditation used by yogis to access a state called "conscious deep sleep." In other words, it lets you experience deep, dreamless sleep while remaining awake.

Because yoga nidra is so good for reducing tension and anxiety, one of the benefits appears to be improved and more peaceful sleep. The best introduction is to find a class where the teacher reads the yoga nidra meditation to you; alternatively, there are some excellent recordings available online.

Deep breathing exercise

This simple breathing exercise is relaxing for the body and mind, so it is particularly helpful before you go to sleep. You can do it lying down in bed.

- Let your arms relax on each side of your body and keep your legs about hips' width apart. Initially, take just a few gentle deep breaths, inhaling through your nose and exhaling through your mouth, mindful of filling and emptying your lungs completely.

- Now take a deep inhale through your nose for a count of four. You might create a soft sound as you do so that also helps to soothe and relax you. Hold the breath at the top of the inhale for a count of four, then exhale through your nose for a count of four.

- On the next breath, inhale for a count of six, hold for a count of six, and exhale for a count of six. And the breath after that, inhale, hold, and exhale for counts of eight. If you can, try building up to counts of ten and twelve.

- To complete the exercise, start reducing the count by two for each breath until you finish with a count of four.

- Now just let go and breathe normally . . .

When you wake

Here are some ideas to help give you an energy boost and sharpen your mental clarity in preparation for the day ahead:

● ● ● Reset your bio clock

Go outside and get fifteen minutes of sunlight when you wake up to reset your natural circadian rhythms.

● ● ● Meditate

Many people don't meditate because they are worried that they can't get their minds to be quiet and still. If this sounds familiar to you, don't worry. It's not necessary for your mind to be still when you meditate; in fact, especially at the beginning, your mind will probably be very active. Trying to stop your thoughts will feel like wrestling a crocodile! The key to meditation is to be okay with the thoughts being there and to keep your focus on your breathing. The thoughts will just come and go. Here's a simple way to meditate:

- ● ● ● Find a comfortable place you can sit with your back straight.
- ● ● ● Lower your gaze and bring your focus and attention inward.
- ● ● ● Take three long deep breaths, inhaling through your nose and exhaling through your mouth.

continued on following page

● ● ● As you settle you can close your eyes.

● ● ● Completely exhale for one breath—this will reset your natural breathing pattern.

● ● ● Focus on your natural breath, without needing to change it unless you want to.

● ● ● Let the thoughts come and go.

● ● ● When you notice you have drifted and got caught on a thought, put your attention back on your breathing.

● ● ● Remain seated and focused on your breath for ten, fifteen, or twenty minutes (you can build up to more if you want over time).

● ● ● When you have finished, rub your hands together to generate some heat.

● ● ● Hold your hand over your face and eyes, and slowly open your eyes beneath your hands.

● ● ● **Dance**
Dancing for five to ten minutes to your favorite music will have you bursting into your day completely refreshed and reenergized.

Breathing exercise

In Chinese traditions, there is a revitalizing deep-breathing exercise called Upholding Heaven. Here's how to do it:

- Stand with your feet comfortably apart and your arms at your sides. Keep your eyes open.

- Focus on your breath. Slowly breathe in through your nose, filling your belly with air, while raising your arms out to the sides and up above your head.

- Interlock your fingers with your palms facing down.

- Keep your fingers interlocked while rotating your hands so that your palms face the sky.

- Look up at the back of your hands.

- Inhale more, stretching upward as if you are wanting to push your hands up toward heaven.

- Keep focusing on your breath. Exhale while you let your arms float down to your sides. Keep exhaling, letting go of your tension. Relax your shoulders.

- Repeat the whole exercise at least another five times. Focus on your breathing, letting your body relax each time you exhale.

movement

The toll of modern-day living is easy to read in our bodies. If you live an average lifestyle, with a diet high in processed foods and a schedule packed with responsibilities that leaves little time for exercising or relaxing, then over time you might start to notice dark circles under your eyes, dry skin, or find you carry excess weight around your middle. You might experience uncontrollable urges to eat or no appetite at all, or simply have a lethargy for life. These symptoms, among others, can often be an indication that one or more of your vital organs is under stress. When our organs are stressed, qi, the life force within them, reduces. For example, if you are someone who gives a lot to other people, it's not uncommon for the adrenal and kidney energies to become depleted. The good news is that it is possible to cultivate this energy from within you—in fact, nowadays it is essential to do so.

We've looked at how to do this with rest and nourishment; now we will explore how movement can raise your energy levels, too. Exercises, such as running, weight lifting, and even most types of yoga are yang, while yin yoga, qi gong, and tai chi are yin. As one article put it, "To the yin-style exerciser, exercise is a cup of camomile tea, to the yang, it's a triple espresso." The Western yang approach to exercise, which is goal-oriented and intensive, comes with the assumption that exertion equals results. This isn't wrong, but, as you know, yin and yang energies don't operate in extremes—they want to be balanced, and focusing on only yang forms of exercise creates an imbalance.

Yin practices, such as qi gong and tai chi, have a powerful holistic effect on both the body and the mind and are great for building qi. These ancient Chinese traditions involve performing sequences of fluid, smooth, deliberately slow movements that are synchronized with the inhalations and exhalations of the breath to cultivate energy and power in the body. They are forms of exercise, but they can also been seen as practices to be mastered over time to strengthen the body and to train you to master your mind. As your mind becomes stiller, the qi rises up in your body. There is a great subtlety to these types of training, but don't be misled by this. When you strip back complexity, there is an innate power in simplicity.

Emotional flow

In the qi-building types of movement, there is an emphasis on both moving the body and being able to manage your mind. Do you ever experience a busy mind? You're not alone. Often people find it hard to still their minds, as thoughts rush through like a freight train at uncontrollable speed. When you listen closely to your inner mind chatter, you might notice that it is thinking ahead of time. An anxious mind can freewheel into the future, sometimes thinking about ramifications of work decisions and working out permutations of personal choices that could be three, six, or even twelve months and beyond into your future. There is undoubtedly good sense in planning ahead, but when your thinking is constantly out of control with worry about the future, that's a different experience. After all, in reality, we can only ever deal with what is right here, right now.

When our minds drag us far into the future (or back into the past), there is a separation from the body that can occur—a split. Your body is in the here and now, but your mind is in a different place altogether. When this happens, it blocks your ability to flow with what is. You might experience an increase of anxiety or fear and feel paralyzed or make hasty decisions. This prevents you from being able to tune into your own instincts, your intuition, and it stems your natural flow. The Pause is about learning how to trust your body, strip back the overthinking, and come back to the here and now. The key to creating this type of flow is your breath. Breath is the pathway between your mind and body. Becoming more conscious of your breathing through practices such as qi gong, tai chi, and yin yoga will support you to connect more deeply with yourself. This type of conscious movement enables you to reconnect with your body and build an inner emotional strength.

micro pauses

● ● ●

Do you find your diary is crammed from the moment you start work? Perhaps you're already checking emails over breakfast, or squeezing in calls on your commute to the office. You're not alone, but being constantly turned on like this can wreak havoc with your stress levels, and, before you know it, you're on a road to burnout. There are ways to minimize this risk. You often hear people talk about "living in the moment." Being in the moment is just you taking a few seconds or minutes to recognize what's happening at that exact time. Micro pauses are simple ways for you to rebalance when you need it.

Enjoy these micro pauses as part of your daily devotions; they are lifelong practices that can grow with you over time. Notice how you are each time you show up and, equally, how much resistance you have to showing up. The aim is not to be perfect but to be awake, conscious, and observant of yourself.

Five micro pauses that will take you less than two minutes

Micro pause one

If you want to gain perspective, look out at the horizon.

When you are feeling busy and stressed, your attention
naturally goes inward and closes down your creativity.
Go and stand by a window, letting your attention move
outward to the horizon. Breathe as you do this and let fresh
perspectives come to you. Let your eyes relax and soften and
let your gaze gently expand. Stay here for a couple of minutes
(you can pretend you're being wise and creative and deep
in thought, generating a masterful idea). Take your breath
in through your nose and down into your belly. This will
have you rebalanced before you know it.

micro pauses

● ● ● ●

Micro pause two

If you want to reduce stress, drink more water.

That band of tension around your head isn't always stress; it can be dehydration as the cells in your brain shrink from lack of fluids.

Keep a bottle of water with you and drink more than you need. If you find yourself going to the bathroom more to begin with, this is another sign you are dehydrated—drink up and your body will rebalance.

Micro pause three

If you want to feel calm, inhale lavender oil.

Lavender is one of the most versatile oils to have in your destress kit. Put a couple of drops of oil into your palms, rub together, then inhale deeply for instant calm. Add a few drops to your bath with a carrier oil, or sprinkle on your pillow to help you sleep at night.

micro pauses

● ● ●

Micro pause four

If you want to find balance, take three deep breaths.

When you feel anxious, your chest tightens and your breath becomes shallow; the resulting lack of oxygen makes you feel even more anxious.

In these moments, it helps to breathe, and then breathe again more deeply. Breathing reconnects you to your body, reduces anxiety, and lets you come back to the here and now. Close your eyes or choose a focus point and take a deep breath, in through your nose and right down into your belly, exhaling gently through your mouth. Repeat this three times (or more) to rebalance.

Micro pause five

Find yourself a special container or jar. It can be beautiful or practical, big or small. Whatever feels right for you.

Over the course of a year, add little notes every time something happens that you are grateful for. Anything that is memorable, makes you smile, or warms your heart.

In twelve months' time, you will have a gorgeous gift to open and reflect on all the precious moments that make up your year.

micro pauses

● ● ●

Five micro pauses that will take you less than ten minutes

Micro pause six
If you want to lift your mood, keep a gratitude diary.

Usually when energy is stuck, we have an experience of lack, a feeling that there is something missing. There isn't enough of something we need or want—love, time, understanding, money. The easiest way to get unstuck and back into flow is gratitude. Being grateful for what is truly present. Opening your heart and mind to how rich your life really is.

Like meditation, it's a practice. Some days you will see an abundance of things to feel grateful for, other days it will look like a barren desert—that's okay. If you look closely enough, turn over the stone, you will find something you can appreciate—gratitude is always available to you, even if it's simply being grateful for this breath. And the next. And the next.

Keep a journal in which you express three things you are grateful for each day. They can be people, events, experiences, or qualities. From the simple to the sublime!

micro pauses

● ● ●

Micro pause seven

If you want your day to get off to a good start, prepare the night before.

Create a more relaxed morning by taking ten minutes before bed preparing what you need for the next day.

Soak some breakfast oats, prepare your coffee, set out your supplements, pack your lunch, lay out your clothes, charge your phone, and have your keys somewhere that you can find them easily.

Micro pause eight

If you want to create more free time, book in "white space."

If you find you spend your days rushing from one thing to the next with no space to pause, it's time to rethink how you manage your diary.

Block out "white space"—time in your diary with nothing scheduled. This could be at weekends when you don't make any social commitments, or at work where you leave yourself white space at the beginning of your day, between meetings, at lunchtime, or on Friday afternoons.

Space between meetings is particularly beneficial—your brain and body aren't designed to jam too much information in each day. When you have white space scheduled, it's entirely up to you how you use it—for creative thinking, planning your next week, or prepping for an important meeting. The idea is that it's your time.

micro pauses

● ● ●

Micro pause nine

To develop your focus, practice a standing meditation for a few minutes each day.

To get started, find a place where you can stand undisturbed for five minutes.

Stand with your legs hips' width apart.

Ground yourself down through your legs, placing two-thirds of your weight on the balls of your feet. Tip your sacrum under, keeping your spine straight and your arms relaxed by your side. Breathe deeply down into your abdomen and let yourself relax completely as you stand. You will know you are doing it properly when you can stand with no tension in your body. Stand like this for five minutes to start with. As you get stronger and your mind becomes stiller, you will be able to stand for longer periods. Build up by five minutes at a time. If you have access to a yard or a park, doing this meditation while standing barefoot on the grass will add to its power.

Micro pause ten

If you want to restore your qi, the first step is to pause and slow down. The simplest way to do this is to sit quietly for five minutes and follow your breath. You can do this at any time, but keep your eyes open if you are in a situation, such as driving, that requires it.

Training your mind to be still by focusing on your breath is important, because, each time your mind wanders, your qi or energy is moving away from sourcing your inner experience. Essentially, your qi will go where your mind goes. The more you can train your mind to be still and let yourself go into stillness, the more you can keep your qi moving in your body.

The aim of the exercise is to complete ten cycles of breath, and to maintain total focus on the breath for those ten cycles.

So let's try one cycle. You can do this standing or sitting and with your eyes open or closed, as the situation dictates.

Let your spine be straight and your head rest gently on your shoulders with your chin lifted slightly. Let go of your shoulders and stomach so they relax.

Slowly take a breath in through your nose and follow it as it travels up over your forehead and over the crown of your head, down through your neck, and all the way down your spine.

continued on following pages

micro pauses
● ● ●

Let the breath fill your belly and travel up through your chest, then exhale gently through your mouth as if you were blowing out a candle.

Then shake your body off gently and notice how you feel.

That was the practice cycle.

Now you'll be doing ten consecutive breaths.

As you repeat the cycle, you may notice a pause between your inhale and exhale. Don't worry about this gap—it's important because it's the space where your qi rises.

If your mind wanders, simply bring it back to your breath.

If ten cycles sounds too many, try five; if it sounds too few, try fifteen or twenty. Whatever is comfortable for you.

Take your time. There's no rush to do this.

Remember that the aim is to come back to your breath each time your mind wanders.

When you finish your cycles, take some time to sit or stand and notice your body. Be aware of the experience you are having.

This is a powerful practice that you can do daily.

As you get used to the number of cycles and can maintain your focus on your breath without your mind wandering, you can increase them by another five.

This practice will help train your mind to become more still. As your breathing slows and deepens, the body naturally moves into the parasympathetic nervous system. This is a natural, relaxed state for your body to be, sometimes described as "rest and digest."

micro pauses

● ● ●

Bonus pause

This one requires more time but is totally worth it. Every now and then, give yourself a guilt-free day off. Plan to do the things that make you most happy. Walk in the woods, curl up in front of the fire with a good book, paint, dance, spend time with friends, or simply do nothing.

cutting down on technology

I don't receive a huge volume of email, but I do give each reply time and thought. I also write from my laptop and not my smartphone unless it's a brief response. Checking email on my phone causes a distraction, splits my energy, and reduces my focus on the person or activity in front of me.

When I first confined email to my laptop, it felt like a big risk, but the rewards have been great. I have more headspace and am more present without email on my phone. The longer I have left it, the less I miss it. I also took the next step: I bought an alarm clock and have banished my smartphone, tablet, and laptop from my bedroom. I haven't looked back. If you would like to be more mindful and less distracted day to day, here are three tips that can help:

- Set your smartphone to airplane mode at night. If you're not already doing this and you use your phone as an alarm clock, please take this one small step so you're not energetically receiving emails through the night.

- Turn your email to offline for set periods of your day. Check and reply to messages once in the morning, and again if you need to in the afternoon or evening. Remember, the fewer you send, the fewer you receive.

- I know some of you have tens of thousands of emails. It's an energy drain. Imagine them as letters on your desk—you wouldn't function. Get rid of junk and clean up your inbox using the wonderful Unroll.Me app.

summary

If you think you are heading toward an enforced pause, here are some ideas to help you to slow down and breathe again:

- **Technology**—Reduce the cortisol spikes in your body by:
  - Removing all alerts from your phone.
  - Deleting social media apps from your phone.
  - If you're feeling bold, you can also turn email off on your phone—you will survive, I promise!

- **Nutrition**—Fupport your overall system by:
  - Eating less sugar, gluten, and dairy.
  - Increasing your daily intake of water.
  - Cutting out caffeine (remember it's hidden in some carbonated beverages and is also in chocolate).

- **Reflection**—Let yourself slow down and reflect on the signs life is giving you by:
  - Journaling daily, even if it's just a paragraph.
  - Writing down the dreams you have at night can have a powerful effect.
  - Working closely with a good coach, therapist, or body worker.
  - Regularly spending time in Nature.

I'm ever grateful to have been taught how to read the signs of my life, to be able to enquire and get the message. I'm discovering I don't always get it right, but my life has undoubtedly changed as a result.

❝ Listen to the wind, it talks
Listen to the silence, it speaks
Listen to your heart, it knows. ❞

Native American proverb

About the author

Danielle Marchant has a history as a successful executive coach in the corporate industry, working with top-level executives at companies, such as HSBC, McKinsey Unilever, and SAP. She has more than thirteen years' experience working with leaders in twenty different countries. After learning that goals and ambitions could be just as happily and successfully achieved when simply letting the body and mind pause, she adapted her coaching style with both personal and corporate clients to flow instead of fight against the ups and downs of life.

"I lived and worked in Singapore running two businesses and life was anything but quiet, in fact, it was fun and fabulous, until one day life gave me a wake-up call. I had pushed myself beyond my limits and my body could no longer sustain the breakneck pace. After recovering from burnout, I quit my job and returned to the UK, and through this experience my business was born."

acknowledgments

Not just for this book, but for shaping my life, thanks goes to my teachers, friends, and family—you have each shown me my way through your way, thank you. To anyone who has ever allowed me to work alongside them, thank you for trusting me. To my team and the light workers who walk this path with me, thank you for your devotion, your presence is so needed in this world at this time. To Hannah, Prue, Avni, and Zoe—my original Coeur Four, your love helps me to burn brighter in the world. To my editor Kate, who understood the Pause better than I did from the beginning, and who had the gift and grace to help birth this book—hank you. Huge thanks to the team at Octopus for your love of words, your passion, creativity, and faith in this book. To ASD for letting me know what love is, I am forever grateful. To life, the forces that guide us—thank you for your mysterious ways. Finally, for anyone who has had to fight in their lives, this book is for you. May you find the flow that is, for all of us, ever present.